The Prayers That Shaped America

The Prayers That Shaped America

DR. CHUCK HARDING

~

PASTOR T. MICHAEL CREED

Copyright © 2014 by Awake America Inc.
All Scripture quotations are taken from the King James Version.
Special emphasis in verses is added.

First printing in Feb. 2014
Second printing in Nov. 2014

by Bible and Literature Missionary Foundation,
a ministry of Victory Baptist Church, Shelbyville, TN 37160

All rights reserved. No part of this book may be reproduced, stored in a retrieval system, or transmitted in any form or by any means – electronic, mechanical, photocopy, recording or otherwise – without written permission of the publisher, except for brief quotations in printed reviews.

Awake America Inc.
113 Second St. North East
Washington, D.C. 20002

Cover design by Alan Salway
Edited by Valerie Creed and Jo Harding
Special thanks to Pat Deason type-setting

Special thanks to the Library of Congress for their historic documentation. The authors and publication team have put every effort to give proper credit to quotes and thoughts that are not original with the authors. It is not our intent to claim originality with any quote or thought that could not readily be tied to an original source.

ISBN 978-0-9789325-9-6

ISBN 978-0-9789325-9-6

Printed in the United States of America

Contents

Introduction ix

1. Patriarchs' Prayers 1
2. Preachers' Prayers 19
3. Pilgrims' Prayers 67
4. Political Prayers 81
5. Presidential Prayers 101
6. Present-Day Prayers 151
7. Patterns for Prayers 165
8. Personal Prayers 179
9. Promissory Prayer 211

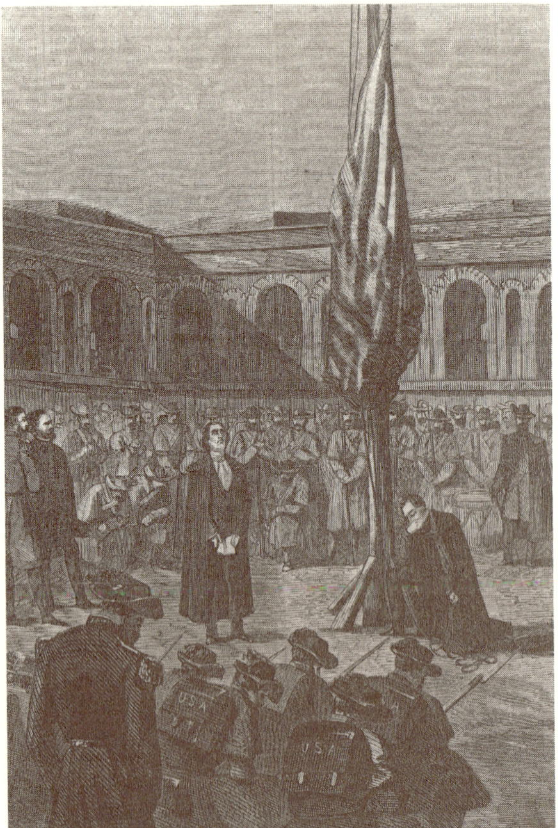
U.S.A
U.S.A

Our Father which art in heaven,
Hallowed be thy name.
Thy kingdom come.
Thy will be done in earth, as it is in heaven.
Give us this day our daily bread.
And forgive us our debts, as we forgive our debtors.
And lead us not into temptation,
but deliver us from evil:
For thine is the kingdom, and the power,
and the glory, for ever. Amen.
~Matthew 6:9-13

Introduction

Prayer and the governing of our Nation have been forever etched in our Country's history. The first order of business for the Continental Congress was a call to prayer on September 6, 1774. The British troops were attacking Boston and the response of our legislative leadership was to bow and humbly petition the Author of Liberty for His protection and providential guidance.

During the War for Independence individual leaders and Congress itself proclaimed days of prayer and fasting throughout the land. There is no other way to explain why we won the War for Independence aside from the divine intervention of God that was garnered by the people of America and their leaders.

The story of prayer in America is one of the most remarkable aspects in world history. Prayer played a critical role in preserving our Country through trying times and preparing our Country to become a world leader for the elevation, welfare, and liberty of mankind.

The mighty elements of prayer have shaped our Nation's character and guided its path from the inception of our Nation to the present day. Prayers have girded our military for valor and guided our public leaders for sacrificial service. Prayer has filled the hearts of Americans with hope and courage and has given us the will to continue. In a world of trouble and turmoil, prayer is the anchor that keeps us grounded in the principles that made this Nation great.

Prayer must not be relegated to the pages of this book. It is our prayer that everyone who reads this book will be encouraged to incorporate prayer more effectively in their daily lives for themselves, for their family, for their friends, and for our Nation.

Your friend and servant for God and Country,

Charles Scott Harding
Awake America

Chapter One

Patriarchs' Prayers

When opening the pages of the Holy Bible, which is the Word of God, we are given a glimpse of individuals who fell to their knees and called out to God, Who is the Creator of all that exists. These patriarchs were our forefathers and prominent leaders of God's people, Israel. We find they were people like we are, yet they depended on the Divine power of Almighty God in the affairs of men and nations. As we view their prayers, may we be driven in our time here to this same dependence on God. The Holy Bible entreats us to call on God in prayer.

"Call unto me, and I will answer thee, and shew thee great and mighty things, which thou knowest not" (Jeremiah 33:3).

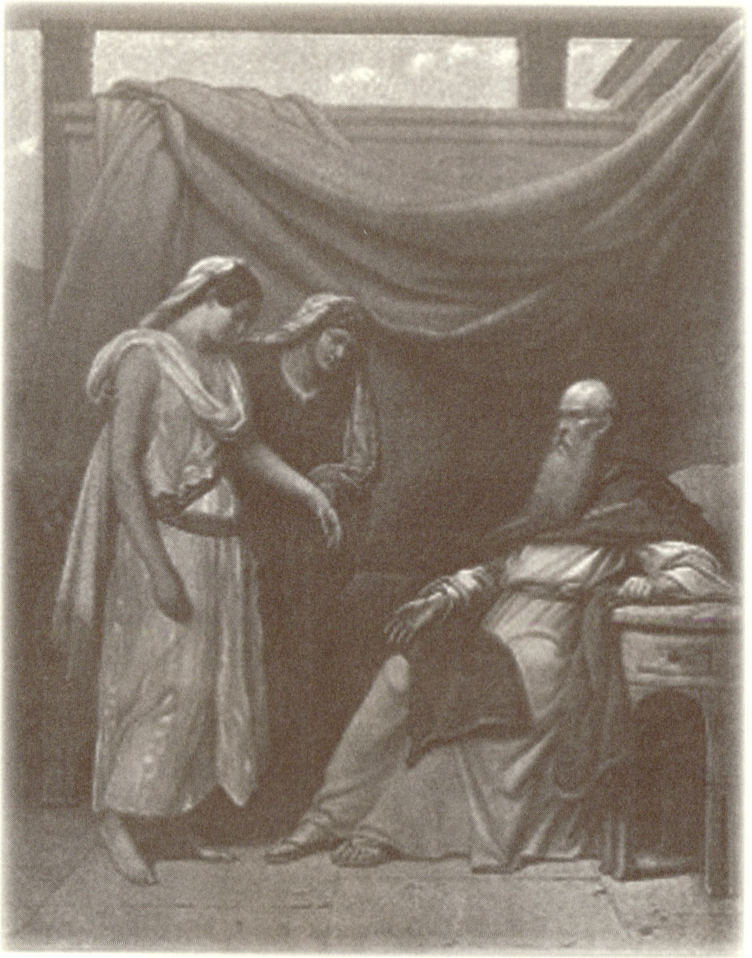

Abraham

Abraham's prayer reveals the nature of man as well as the mercy of God. This prayer shows the humanity of Abraham as he negotiates with God concerning God's judgment on Sodom. We are also given a glimpse to an inside view of how God is willing to have mercy in desperate situations while still keeping His righteous judgment. Abraham believed God.

"And the scripture was fulfilled which saith, Abraham believed God, and it was imputed unto him for righteousness: and he was called the Friend of God" (James 2:23).

"And Abraham drew near, and said, Wilt thou also destroy the righteous with the wicked? Peradventure there be fifty righteous within the city: wilt thou also destroy and not spare the place for the fifty righteous that are therein? That be far from thee to do after this manner, to slay the righteous with the wicked: and that the righteous should be as the wicked, that be far from thee: Shall not the Judge of all the earth do right? And the LORD said, If I find in Sodom fifty righteous within the city, then I will spare all the place for their sakes. And Abraham answered and said, Behold now, I have taken upon me to speak unto the Lord, which am but dust and ashes: Peradventure there shall lack five of the fifty righteous: wilt thou destroy all the city for lack of five? And he said, If I find there forty and five, I will not destroy it. And he spake unto him yet again, and said, Peradventure there shall be forty found there. And he said, I will not do it for forty's sake. And he said unto him, Oh let not the Lord be angry, and I will speak: Peradventure there shall thirty be found there. And he said, I will not do it, if I find thirty there. And he said, Behold now, I have taken upon me to speak unto the Lord: Peradventure there shall be twenty found there. And he said, I will not destroy it for twenty's sake. And he said, Oh let not the Lord be angry, and I will speak yet but this once: Peradventure ten shall be found there. And he said, I will not destroy it for ten's sake" (Genesis 18:23–32).

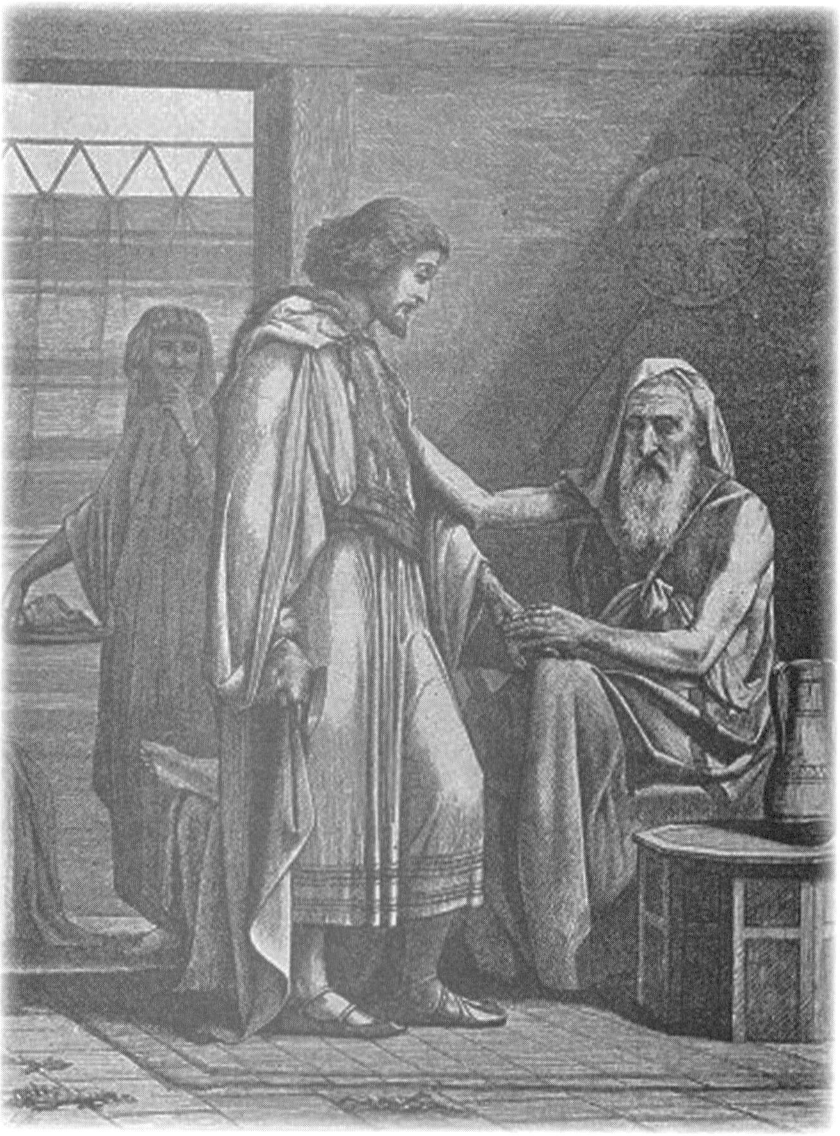

Isaac

Isaac was the covenant child God would give Abraham and Sarah in their old age; Sarah being ninety. Isaac's name was given by God and has the thought of *laughter*. It bares the reaction of his parents to the news of his birth. Isaac and his wife also sought the Lord for a child when all hope seemed lost. Through this prayer, God made Isaac the father of two nations, which has made a great generational impact upon this world.

"And these are the generations of Isaac, Abraham's son: Abraham begat Isaac: And Isaac was forty years old when he took Rebekah to wife, the daughter of Bethuel the Syrian of Padan-aram, the sister to Laban the Syrian. And Isaac intreated the LORD for his wife, because she was barren: and the LORD was intreated of him, and Rebekah his wife conceived. And the children struggled together within her; and she said, If it be so, why am I thus? And she went to inquire of the LORD. And the LORD said unto her, Two nations are in thy womb, and two manner of people shall be separated from thy bowels; and the one people shall be stronger than the other people; and the elder shall serve the younger. And when her days to be delivered were fulfilled, behold, there were twins in her womb. And the first came out red, all over like an hairy garment; and they called his name Esau. And after that came his brother out, and his hand took hold on Esau's heel; and his name was called Jacob: and Isaac was threescore years old when she bare them" (Genesis 25:19–26).

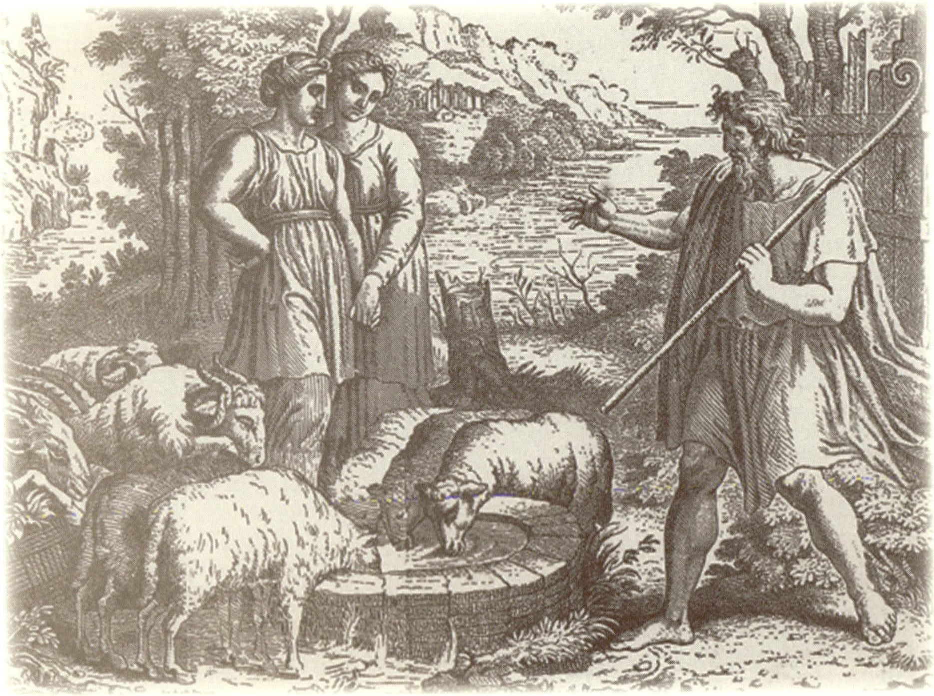

Jacob

Jacob, named Israel by God, was a man who wanted God's blessings at any cost. Though Jacob made many mistakes, he is introduced as a man of faith in Hebrews 11:21. In Genesis, he is found praying for protection from Esau, his brother, from whom he stole the birthright.

"And God said unto him, Thy name is Jacob: thy name shall not be called any more Jacob, but Israel shall be thy name: and he called his name Israel" (Genesis 35:10).

"By faith Jacob, when he was a dying, blessed both the sons of Joseph; and worshipped, leaning upon the top of his staff" (Hebrews 11:21).

"And Jacob said, O God of my father Abraham, and God of my father Isaac, the LORD which saidst unto me, Return unto thy country, and to thy kindred, and I will deal well with thee: I am not worthy of the least of all the mercies, and of all the truth, which thou hast shewed unto thy servant; for with my staff I passed over this Jordan; and now I am become two bands. Deliver me, I pray thee, from the hand of my brother, from the hand of Esau: for I fear him, lest he will come and smite me, and the mother with the children. And thou saidst, I will surely do thee good, and make thy seed as the sand of the sea, which cannot be numbered for multitude. And he lodged there that same night; and took of that which came to his hand a present for Esau his brother" (Genesis 32:9–13).

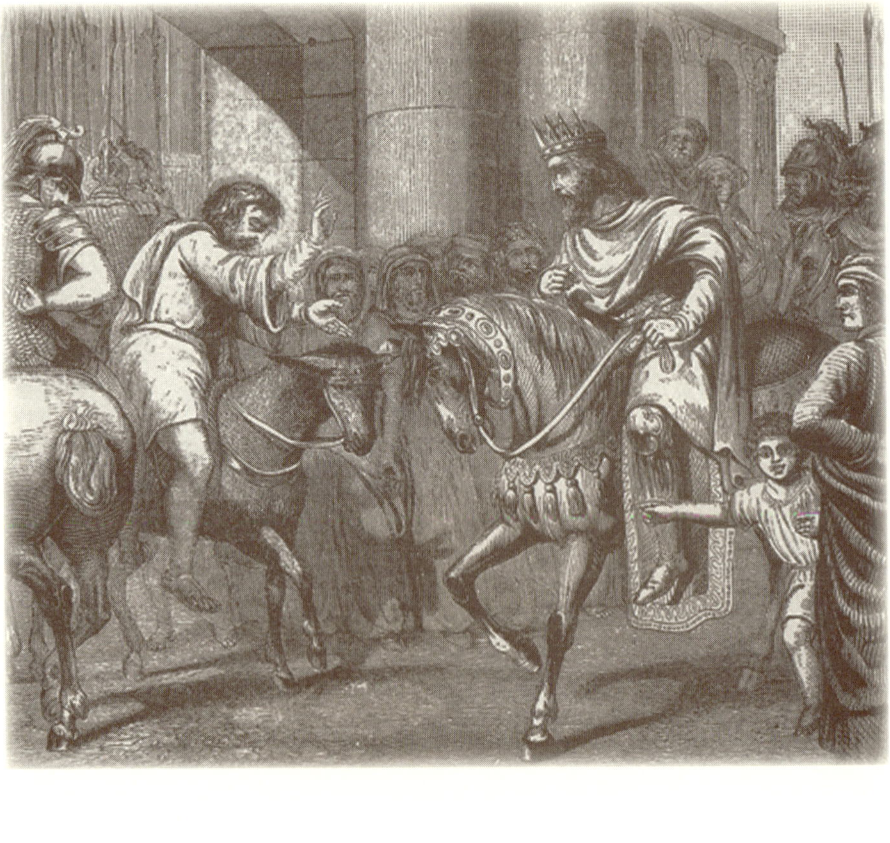

David

King David is often referred to as the Psalmist in the Holy Bible. He constantly cried out to God for protection and provision, and many times simply for fellowship. Psalm 86 is one such prayer of the Psalmist revealing the desires of a man after God's own heart, and David was chosen by God to be King because of this attribute. David replaced King Saul who sought after the favor of man.

"But now thy kingdom shall not continue: the LORD hath sought him a man after his own heart, and the LORD hath commanded him to be captain over his people, because thou hast not kept that which the LORD commanded thee" (1 Samuel 13:14).

"And when he had removed him, he raised up unto them David to be their king; to whom also he gave testimony, and said, I have found David the son of Jesse, a man after mine own heart, which shall fulfil all my will" (Acts 13:22).

"Bow down thine ear, O LORD, hear me: For I am poor and needy. Preserve my soul; for I am holy: O thou my God, save thy servant that trusteth in thee. Be merciful unto me, O Lord: For I cry unto thee daily. Rejoice the soul of thy servant: For unto thee, O Lord, do I lift up my soul. For thou, Lord, art good, and ready to forgive; And plenteous in mercy unto all them that call upon thee. Give ear, O LORD, unto my prayer; And attend to the voice of my supplications. In the day of my trouble I will call upon thee: For thou wilt answer me. Among the gods there is none like unto thee, O Lord; Neither are there any works like unto thy works. All nations whom thou hast made shall come and worship before thee, O Lord; And shall glorify thy name. For thou art great, and doest wondrous things: Thou art God alone. Teach me thy way, O LORD; I will walk in thy truth: Unite my heart to fear thy name. I will praise thee, O Lord my God, with all my heart: And I will glorify thy name for evermore. For great is thy mercy toward me: And thou hast delivered my soul from the lowest hell. O God, the proud are risen against me, and the assemblies of violent men have sought after my soul; And have not set thee before them. But thou, O Lord, art a God full of compassion, and gracious, Longsuffering, and plenteous in mercy and truth. O turn unto me, and have mercy upon me; Give thy strength unto thy servant, And save the son of thine handmaid. Shew me a token for good; That they which hate me may see it, and be ashamed: Because thou, LORD, hast holpen me, and comforted me" (Psalm 86:1–17).

Solomon

King Solomon, the son of King David, was asked by God, "What shall I give thee?" Solomon's response was a request for wisdom to discern between good and bad in governing the people of Israel. This request honored the Lord, hence Solomon has been called the wisest king of Israel. When a visiting queen had seen Solomon's kingdom, she responded with these words,

"And she said to the king, It was a true report which I heard in mine own land of thine acts, and of thy wisdom: Howbeit I believed not their words, until I came, and mine eyes had seen it: and, behold, the one half of the greatness of thy wisdom was not told me: for thou exceedest the fame that I heard" (2 Chronicles 9:5–6).

"And Solomon loved the LORD, walking in the statutes of David his father: only he sacrificed and burnt incense in high places. And the king went to Gibeon to sacrifice there; for that was the great high place: a thousand burnt offerings did Solomon offer upon that altar. In Gibeon the LORD appeared to Solomon in a dream by night: and God said, Ask what I shall give thee. And Solomon said, Thou hast shewed unto thy servant David my father great mercy, according as he walked before thee in truth, and in righteousness, and in uprightness of heart with thee; and thou hast kept for him this great kindness, that thou hast given him a son to sit on his throne, as it is this day. And now, O LORD my God, thou hast made thy servant king instead of David my father: and I am but a little child: I know not how to go out or come in. And thy servant is in the midst of thy people which thou hast chosen, a great people, that cannot be numbered nor counted for multitude. Give therefore thy servant an understanding heart to judge thy people, that I may discern between good and bad: for who is able to judge this thy so great a people? And the speech pleased the Lord, that Solomon had asked this thing. And God said unto him, Because thou hast asked this thing, and hast not asked for thyself long life; neither hast asked riches for thyself, nor hast asked the life of thine enemies; but hast asked for thyself understanding to discern judgment; Behold, I have done according to thy words: lo, I have given thee a wise and an understanding heart; so that there was none like thee before thee, neither after thee shall any arise like unto thee. And I have also given thee that which thou hast not asked, both riches, and honour: so that there shall not be any among the kings like unto thee all thy days. And if thou wilt walk in my ways, to keep my statutes and my commandments, as thy father David did walk, then I will lengthen thy days. And Solomon awoke; and, behold, it was a dream. And he came to Jerusalem, and stood before the ark of the covenant of the LORD, and offered up burnt offerings, and offered peace offerings, and made a feast to all his servants" (1 Kings 3:1–15).

Jehoshaphat

Jehoshaphat, king of Judah, found his kingdom being attacked by a federation of nations from the north. The first thing this Godly king did was to depend on God's divine promises by running to God in prayer for protection. God's answer came in 2 Chronicles 20:15, "Thus saith the Lord unto you, Be not afraid or dismayed by reason of this great multitude; for the battle is not yours, but God's." Jehoshaphat was given a great victory without raising a single sword.

"And Jehoshaphat stood in the congregation of Judah and Jerusalem, in the house of the LORD, before the new court, And said, O LORD God of our fathers, art not thou God in heaven? and rulest not thou over all the kingdoms of the heathen? and in thine hand is there not power and might, so that none is able to withstand thee? Art not thou our God, who didst drive out the inhabitants of this land before thy people Israel, and gavest it to the seed of Abraham thy friend for ever? And they dwelt therein, and have built thee a sanctuary therein for thy name, saying, If, when evil cometh upon us, as the sword, judgment, or pestilence, or famine, we stand before this house, and in thy presence, (for thy name is in this house,) and cry unto thee in our affliction, then thou wilt hear and help. And now, behold, the children of Ammon and Moab and mount Seir, whom thou wouldest not let Israel invade, when they came out of the land of Egypt, but they turned from them, and destroyed them not; Behold, I say, how they reward us, to come to cast us out of thy possession, which thou hast given us to inherit. O our God, wilt thou not judge them? for we have no might against this great company that cometh against us; neither know we what to do: but our eyes are upon thee" (2 Chronicles 20:5–12).

"And they rose early in the morning, and went forth into the wilderness of Tekoa: and as they went forth, Jehoshaphat stood and said, Hear me, O Judah, and ye inhabitants of Jerusalem; Believe in the LORD your God, so shall ye be established; believe his prophets, so shall ye prosper. And when he had consulted with the people, he appointed singers unto the LORD, and that should praise the beauty of holiness, as they went out before the army, and to say, Praise the LORD; for his mercy endureth for ever. And when they began to sing and to praise, the LORD set ambushments against the children of Ammon, Moab, and mount Seir, which were come against Judah; and they were smitten. For the children of Ammon and Moab stood up against the inhabitants of mount Seir, utterly to slay and destroy them: and when they had made an end of the inhabitants of Seir, every one helped to destroy another. And when Judah came toward the watch tower in the wilderness, they looked unto the multitude, and, behold, they were dead bodies fallen to the earth, and none escaped" (2 Chronicles 20:20–24).

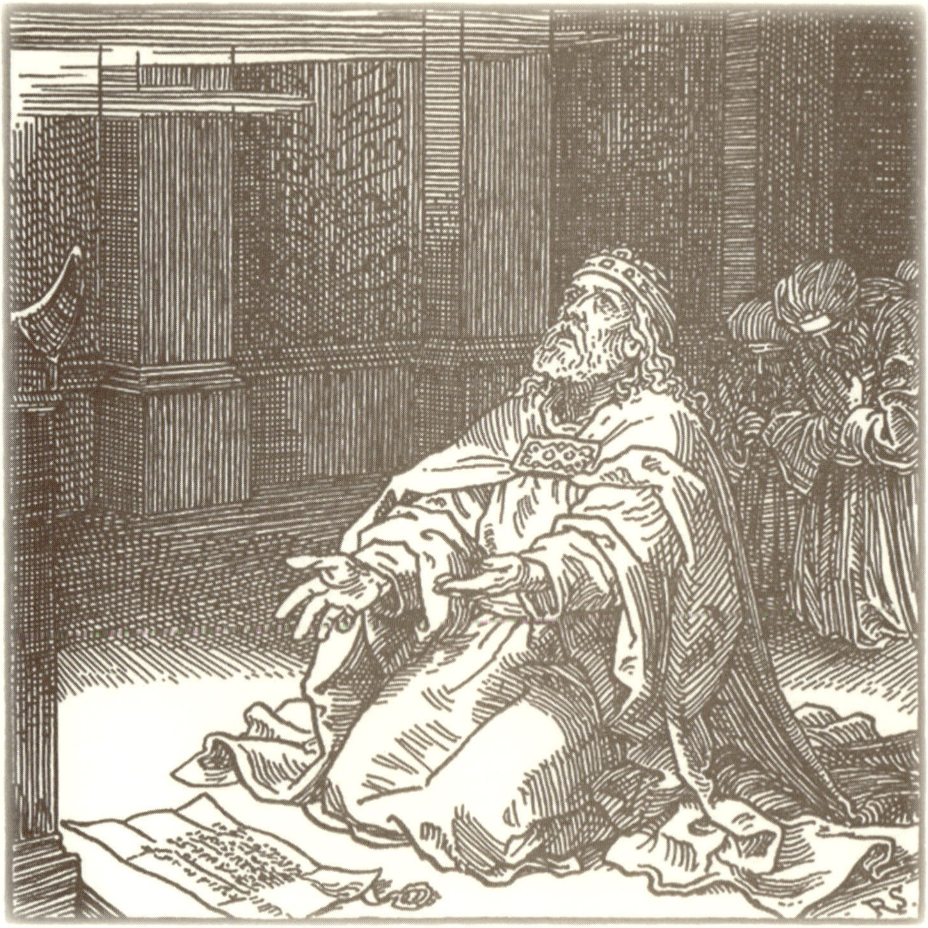

Hezekiah

Hezekiah was a king of Judah who prayed for God's protection, and God defeated King Sennacherib and the Assyrian army. The God of the Holy Bible will protect His children according to His will and for His glory. God blessed the nation of Judah because Hezekiah understood God was their true King.

"And Hezekiah received the letter of the hand of the messengers, and read it: and Hezekiah went up into the house of the LORD, and spread it before the LORD. And Hezekiah prayed before the LORD, and said, O LORD God of Israel, which dwellest between the cherubims, thou art the God, even thou alone, of all the kingdoms of the earth; thou hast made heaven and earth. LORD, bow down thine ear, and hear: open, LORD, thine eyes, and see: and hear the words of Sennacherib, which hath sent him to reproach the living God. Of a truth, LORD, the kings of Assyria have destroyed the nations and their lands, And have cast their gods into the fire: for they were no gods, but the work of men's hands, wood and stone: therefore they have destroyed them. Now therefore, O LORD our God, I beseech thee, save thou us out of his hand, that all the kingdoms of the earth may know that thou art the LORD God, even thou only" (2 Kings 19:14-19).

"Therefore thus saith the LORD concerning the king of Assyria, He shall not come into this city, Nor shoot an arrow there, Nor come before it with shield, Nor cast a bank against it. By the way that he came, by the same shall he return, And shall not come into this city, saith the LORD. For I will defend this city, to save it, For mine own sake, and for my servant David's sake. And it came to pass that night, that the angel of the LORD went out, and smote in the camp of the Assyrians an hundred fourscore and five thousand: and when they arose early in the morning, behold, they were all dead corpses. So Sennacherib king of Assyria departed, and went and returned, and dwelt at Nineveh. And it came to pass, as he was worshipping in the house of Nisroch his god, that Adrammelech and Sharezer his sons smote him with the sword: and they escaped into the land of Armenia. And Esarhaddon his son reigned in his stead" (2 Kings 19:32-37).

As we look at the prayers of these great patriarchs, may we understand the need to call out to God for America's families and cities, and for our protection, our wisdom, and our defense. We have a God who will meet these needs.

Chapter Two

Preachers' Prayers

The heroes of the War for Independence were great men. Our founding fathers were educated, talented, cultured, and wealthy yet, they were willing to sacrifice it all. They said to each other "with firm reliance on the protection of divine providence we mutually pledge to each other our lives, our fortunes, and our sacred honor". These men were settled in character and reputation. They could have chosen a life of luxury but they chose liberty instead. Not only for themselves but for the common man. Why were they willing to do such a thing? The reason is these men, these legislative leaders, were the children of the Great Awakening. As young boys they had heard the great men of God preaching sometimes in threat of their lives. These preachers are the unsung heroes of our struggle for liberty for they infused that sacred fire, that sense of duty and sacrificial prayer into the hearts of our forefathers and gave them the resolution of faith to endure against all odds and to win our Independence from the tyranny of Great Britain, and to establish this Constitutional Republic.

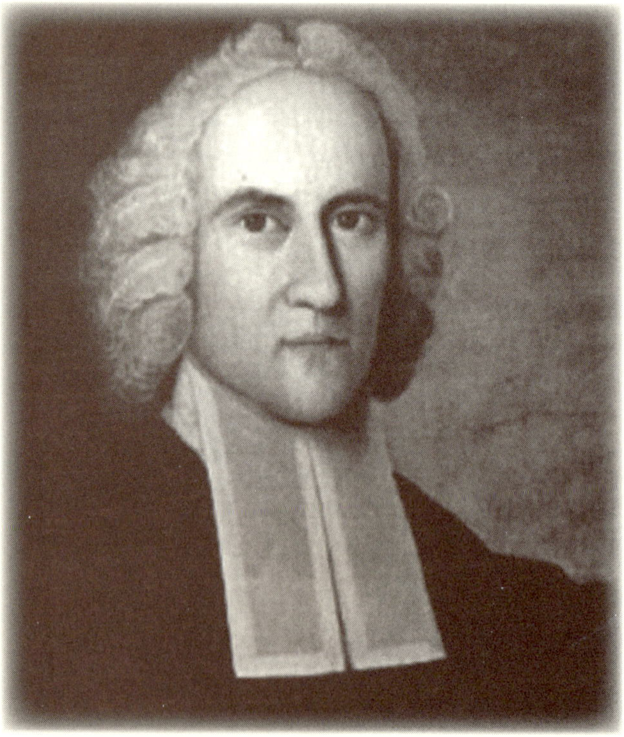

Prayers of the Preachers of the Great Awakening

Jonathan Edwards - Quotes on Prayer

"When we say, "for the sake of" such or such a person, it implies that the thing we speak of will be for the advantage of that person, and that he will get by it. Wherefore, when we pray for grace for the sake of Christ, we should intend thereby to desire God to remember that 'twill be to his Son's joy and happiness; for the bestowment of God's grace upon us was the joy that was set before him, the reward he expected, that made him cheerfully subject himself to such torments."

Jonathan Edwards 1703-1758

"Christ has told us that whatsoever we ask the Father in his name shall be given us. Now by asking in Christ's name, nobody will suppose is meant our saying of it in words, that we ask in Christ's name or for his sake, but that it is something in [the] mind; that we really in our minds are sensible that it must be bestowed through him if at all, that we ben't fit for it any other way, and that through him it may be bestowed. That which is necessary in prayer is necessary in faith; for prayer is only the particular exercise and expression of our faith before God."

Jonathan Edwards 1703-1758

"When God is about to bestow some great blessing on his church, it is often his manner, in the first place, so to order things in his providence as to shew his church their great need of it, and to bring 'em into distress for want of it, and so put 'em upon crying earnestly to him for it."

Jonathan Edwards 1703-1758

"The smoke of" Christ's "sacrifice has perfumed the souls of believers and has made them and their prayers and praises sweet in the nostrils of God, so that now he smells a sweet savor in their prayers which were most offensive to him before. The merits of Christ are the incense that ascended out of the angel's hand, accompanied with the prayers of all the saints, whereby they were rendered acceptable to God (Revelation 8:4)."

Jonathan Edwards 1703-1758

"If we, when we stand in need, ask earthly bread of God, he will be much more ready to bestow this upon us than earthly parents are, but much more when we ask [for] the Holy Spirit...Of the more excellent nature any blessing is that we stand in need of, the more ready God is to bestow it in answer to prayer. With men it is otherwise. They are much more ready to bestow things of small nature."

Jonathan Edwards 1703-1758

Jonathan Edwards' Sermon on Prayer

The Most High, A Prayer-Hearing God
Dated January, 1735 (and 1752)

Preached on a fast appointed on the account of epidemical sickness at the eastward of Boston.

Psalms 65:2
O thou that hearest prayer.

Subject: 'Tis the character of the Most High God, that he is a God that answers prayer.

THIS psalm seems to be written, either as a psalm of praise to God for some remarkable answer of prayer, in the bestowment of some public mercy, or else on occasion of some special faith and confidence which David had that his prayer would be answered. It is probable that this mercy bestowed, or expected to be bestowed, was some great public mercy for which David had been very earnest and importunate, and had annexed a vow to his prayer. And that he had vowed to God that if he would grant him his request he would render him praise and glory. — This seems to be the reason why he expresses himself as he does in the first verse of the psalm, "Praise waiteth for thee, O God, in Sion; and unto thee shall the vow be performed," i.e. that praise which I have vowed to give thee, on the answer of my prayer, waiteth for thee, to be given thee as soon as thou shalt have answered my prayer; and the vow which I made to thee shall be performed.

In the verse of the text, there is a prophecy of the glorious times of the gospel, when "all flesh shall come" to the true God, as to *the God who heareth prayer*, which is here mentioned as what distinguishes the true God from the gods to whom the nations prayed and sought, those gods who cannot hear, and cannot answer their prayer. The time was coming when all flesh should come to that God who doth hear prayer. — Hence we gather this doctrine, *that it is the character of the Most High, that he is a God who hears prayer.*

I shall handle this point in the following method:
I. Show that the Most High is a God that hears prayer.
II. That he is eminently such a God.
III. That herein he is distinguished from all false gods.

IV. Give the reasons of the doctrine.

I. The Most High is a God that hears prayer. Though he is infinitely above all and stands in no need of creatures, yet he is graciously pleased to take a merciful notice of poor worms of the dust. He manifests and presents himself as the object of prayer, appears as sitting on a mercy-seat, that men may come to him by prayer. When they stand in need of anything, he allows them to come, and ask it of him, and he is wont to hear their prayers. God in his Word hath given many promises that he will hear their prayers. The Scripture is full of such examples, and in his dispensations towards his church, manifests himself to be a God that hears prayer.

Here it may be inquired what is meant by God's hearing prayer? There are two things implied in it.

First, his *accepting* the supplications of those who pray to him. Their address to him is well taken, he is well-pleased with it. He approves of their asking such mercies as they request of him and approves of their manner of doing it. He accepts of their prayers as an offering to him. He accepts the honor they do him in prayer.

Second, he *acts* agreeably to his acceptance. He sometimes manifests his acceptance of their prayers by special discoveries of his mercy and sufficiency, which he makes to them *in prayer*, or immediately after. While they are praying, he gives them sweet views of his glorious grace, purity, sufficiency, and sovereignty, and enables them, with great quietness, to rest in him, to leave themselves and their prayers with him, submitting to his will and trusting in his grace and faithfulness. Such a manifestation God seems to have made of himself in prayer to *Hannah*, which quieted and composed her mind, and took away her sadness. We read (1 Sam. 1) how earnest she was, and how exercised in her mind, and that she was a woman of a sorrowful spirit. But she came and poured out her soul before God, and spake out of the abundance of her complaint and grief. Then we read that she went away and did eat, and her countenance was no more sad, verse 18, which seems to have been from some refreshing discoveries which God had made of himself to her, to enable her quietly to submit to his will and trust in his mercy, whereby God manifested his acceptance of her. — Not that I conclude persons can hence argue, that the particular thing which they ask will certainly be given them, or that they can particularly foretell from it what God will do in answer to their prayers, any further than he has promised in his Word. Yet God may, and doubtless does, thus testify his acceptance of their prayers, and from hence they may confidently rest in his providence [and] in his merciful ordering and disposing, with respect to the thing which they ask. Again, God manifests his acceptance of their prayers, by *doing* for them agreeably to their needs and supplications. He not only inwardly and spiritually discovers his mercy to their souls by his Spirit, but outwardly by dealing mercifully with them in his providence, in consequence of their prayers, and by causing an agreeableness between his providence and their prayers. — I proceed now,

II. To show that the Most High is *eminently* a God that hears prayer. This appears in several things.

First, in his giving such *free access* to him by prayer. God in his Word manifests himself ready at all times to allow us this privilege. He sits on a throne of grace, and there is no veil to hide this throne and keep us from it. The veil is rent from the top to the bottom. The way is open at all times, and we may go to God as often as we please. Although God be infinitely above us, yet we may come with boldness. Heb. 4:14, 16, "Let us therefore come boldly unto the throne of grace, that we may obtain mercy, and find grace to help in time of need." How wonderful is it that such worms as we should be allowed to come boldly at all times to so great a God! — Thus God indulges all kinds of persons, of all nations. 1 Cor. 1:2, 3, "unto all that in every place call on the name of Jesus Christ our Lord, both theirs and ours; grace be unto you," etc. Yea, God allows the most vile and unworthy: the greatest sinners are allowed to come through Christ. And he not only allows, but encourages and frequently invites them, yea, manifests himself as delighting in being sought to by prayer. Pro. 15:8, "The prayer of the upright is his delight;" and in the Song 2:14, we have Christ saying to the spouse, "O my dove, let me hear they voice; for sweet is they voice." The voice of the saints in prayer is sweet unto Christ, he delights to hear it. He allows them to be earnest and importunate, yea, to the degree as to take no denial, and as it were to give him no rest, and even encouraging them so to do. Isa. 62:6, 7, "Ye that make mention of the Lord, keep not silence, and give him no rest." Thus Christ encourages us, in the parable of the importunate widow and the unjust judge, Luke 18. So, in the parable of the man who went to his friend at midnight, Luke 11:5, etc.

Thus God allowed Jacob to wrestle with him, yea, to be resolute in it, "I will not let thee go, except thou bless me." It is noticed with approbation when men are violent for the kingdom of heaven and take it by force. Thus Christ suffered the blind man to be most importunate and unceasing in his cries to him, Luke 18:38, 39. He continued crying, "Jesus, thou Son of David, have mercy on me." Others who were present rebuked him, that he should hold his peace, looking upon it as too great a boldness and an indecent behavior towards Christ, thus to cry after him as he passed by. But Christ did not rebuke him, but stood and commanded him to be brought unto him, saying, "What wilt thou that I should do to thee?" And when the blind man had told him, Christ graciously granted his request. — The freedom of access that God gives, appears also in allowing us to come to him by prayer for everything we need, both temporal and spiritual, whatever evil we need to be delivered from, or good we would obtain. Phil. 4:6, "Be careful for nothing, but in every thing by prayer and supplication, with thanksgiving, let your requests be made known to God."

Second, that God is eminently of this character, appears in his hearing prayer *so readily*. He often manifests his readiness to hear prayer, by giving an answer so speedily, sometimes while they are yet speaking, and sometimes before they pray, when they only have a design of praying. So ready is God to hear prayer, that he takes notice of the first purpose of praying, and sometimes bestows mercy thereupon. Isa. 65:24, "And it shall come to pass, that before they call, I will answer; and while they are yet speaking, I will hear." We read, that when Daniel was making humble and earnest supplication, God sent an angel to comfort him and to assure him of an answer, Dan. 9:20-24. When God defers for the present to answer the prayer of faith, it is not from any backwardness to answer, but for the good of his people sometimes, that they may be better prepared for the mercy before they receive it, or because another time would be the best and fittest on some other account. And even then, when God seems to delay an answer, the answer is indeed hastened, as in Luke 18:7, 8, "And shall not God avenge his own elect, which cry day and night unto him, though he bear long with them? I tell you, that he will avenge them speedily." Sometimes, when the blessing seems to tarry, God is even then at work to bring it about in the best time and the best manner. Hab. 2:3, "Though it tarry, wait for it; it will come, it will not tarry.

Third, that the Most High is eminently one that hears prayer, appears by his giving so *liberally* in answer to prayer. Jam. 1:5, 6, "If any of you lack wisdom, let him ask of God, who giveth to all liberally, and upbraideth not." Men often show their backwardness to give, both by the scantiness of their gifts and by upbraiding those who ask of them. They will be sure to put them in mind of some faults when they give them anything, but on the contrary, God both gives liberally and upbraids us not with our undeservings. He is plenteous and rich in his communications to those who call upon him. Psa. 86:5, "For thou, Lord, art good, and ready to forgive; and plenteous in mercy unto all them that call upon thee." And Rom. 10:12, "For there is no difference between the Jew and the Greek; for the same Lord over all is rich unto all that call upon him." — Sometimes, God not only gives the thing asked, but he gives them more than is asked. So he did to Solomon. 1 Kin. 3:12, 13, "Behold, I have done according to thy words; lo, I have given thee a wise and an understanding heart, so that there was none like thee, before thee, neither after thee shall any arise like unto thee. And I have also given thee that which thou hast not asked, both riches and honour; so that there shall not be any among the kings like unto thee, all thy days." Yea, God will give more to his people than they can either ask or think, as is implied in Eph. 3:20, "Now unto him that is able to do exceeding abundantly above all that we ask or think."

Fourth, that God is eminently of this character appears by the *greatness* of the things which he has often done in answer to prayer. Thus, when Esau, was coming out against his brother Jacob, with four hundred men, without doubtfully resolved to cut him off, Jacob prayed and God turned the heart of Esau, so that he met Jacob in a very friendly manner, Gen. 32. So in Egypt, at the prayers of Moses, God brought those dreadful plagues, and at his prayer removed them again. When Samson was ready to perish with thirst, he prayed to God, and he brought water out of a dry jaw-bone, for his supply, Jdg. 15:18,19. And when he prayed, after his strength was departed from him, God strengthened him, so as to pull down the temple of Dagon on the Philistines: so that those whom he slew at his death were more than all those whom he slew in his life. — Joshua prayed to God, and said, "Sun, stand thou still upon Gibeon and thou, Moon, in the valley of Ajalon." And God heard his prayer and caused the sun and moon to stand still accordingly. The prophet "Elijah was a man of like passion" with us, "and he prayed earnestly that it might not rain; and it rained not on the earth by the space of three years and six months. And he prayed again, and the heaven gave rain, and the earth brought for her fruit;" as the apostle James observes, Jam. 5:17, 18. So God confounded the army of Zerah, the Ethiopian, of a thousand thousand, in answer to the prayer of Asa, 2 Chr. 14:9, etc. And God sent an angel and slew in one night an hundred and eighty-five thousand men of Sennacherib's army, in answer to Hezekiah's prayer, 2 Kin. 19:14-16,19,35.

Fifth, this truth appears, in that God is, as it were, *overcome* by prayer. When God is displeased by sin, he manifests his displeasure, comes out against us in his providence, and seems to oppose and resist us. In such cases, God is, speaking after the manner of men, overcome by humble and fervent prayer. "The effectual fervent prayer of a righteous man availeth much," Jam. 5:16. It has a great power in it: such a prayer-hearing God is the Most High, that he graciously manifests himself as conquered by it. Thus God appeared to oppose Jacob in what he sought of him. Yet Jacob was resolute and overcame. Therefore God changed his name from Jacob to Israel, for says he, "as a prince thou hast power with God and with men, and hast prevailed," Gen. 32:28. A mighty prince indeed! Hos 12:4, "Yea, he had power over the angel, and prevailed; He wept and made supplication unto him." — When his anger was provoked against Israel, and he appeared to be ready to consume them in his hot displeasure, Moses stood in the gap, and by his humbled and earnest prayer and supplication, averted the stroke of divine vengeance, Exo. 32:9, etc. Num. 14:11, etc.

III. Herein the most high God is *distinguished* from false gods. The true God is the only one of this character. There is no other of whom it may be said, that he *heareth prayer.*

Many of those things that are worshipped as gods are idols made by their worshippers: mere stocks and stones that know nothing. They are indeed made with ears, but they hear not the prayers of them that cry to them. They have eyes, but they see not, etc. Psa. 115:5, 6. — Others, though not the work of men's hands, yet are things *without life.* Thus, many worship the sun, moon, and stars, which though glorious creatures, yet are not capable of knowing anything of the wants and desires of those who pray to them. — Some worship certain kinds of *animals*, as the Egyptians were wont to worship bulls, which though not without life, yet are destitute of that reason whereby they would be capable of knowing the requests of their worshippers. Others worship *devils* instead of the true God. 1 Cor. 10:20, "but I say, that the things which the Gentiles sacrifice, they sacrifice to devils." These, though beings of great power, have not knowledge necessary to capacitate them fully to understand the state, circumstances, necessities, and desires of those who pray to them. But the true God perfectly knows the circumstances of everyone that prays to him throughout the world. Though millions pray to him at once, in different parts of the world, it is no more difficult for him who is infinite in knowledge, to take notice of all than of one alone. God is so perfect in knowledge, that he does not need to be informed by us in order to a knowledge of our wants, for he know what things we need before we ask him. The worshippers of false gods were wont to lift their voices and cry aloud, lest their gods should fail of hearing them, as Elijah tauntingly bid the worshippers of Baal [to] do, 1 Kin. 18:27. But the true God hears the silent petitions of his people. He needs not that we should cry aloud: yea, he knows and perfectly understands when we only pray in our hearts, as Hannah did, 1 Sam. 1:13.

Idols are but vanities and lies: in them is no help. As to power or knowledge, they are nothing. As the apostle says, 1 Cor. 8:4, "An idol is nothing in the world." As to images, they are so far from having power to answer prayer, that they are not able to act, "They have hands, and handle not; feet have they, but they walk not; neither speak they through their throat." They, therefore, that make them and pray to them, are senseless and sottish, and make themselves, as it were, stocks and stones, like unto them: Psa. 115:7, 8, and Jer. 10:5. "They are upright as the palm tree, but speak not; they must needs be borne, because they cannot go. Be not afraid of them; for they cannot do evil; neither also is it in them to do good." As to the hosts of heaven, the sun, moon, and stars: although mankind receive benefit by them, yet they act only by necessity of nature. Therefore they have no power to do anything in answer to prayers. And devils, though worshipped as gods, are not able, if they had disposition, to make those happy who worship them, and [they] can do nothing at all but by divine permission and as subject to the disposal of Divine Providence. When the children of Israel departed from the true God to idols, and yet cried to him in their distress, he reproved them for their folly, by bidding them cry to the gods whom they had served, for deliverance in the time of their tribulation, Jos. 10:14. So God challenges those gods themselves. Isa. 41:23, 24, "Show the things that are to come hereafter, that we may know that ye are gods; yea, do good, or do evil, that we may be dismayed and behold it together. Behold, ye are of nothing, and your work of nought; an abomination is he that chooseth you." — These false gods, instead of helping those who pray to them, cannot help themselves. The devils are miserable tormented spirits. They are bound in chains of darkness for their rebellion against the true God and cannot deliver themselves. Nor have they any more disposition to help mankind than a parcel of hungry wolves or lions would have to protect and help a flock of lambs. And those that worship and pray to them get not their goodwill by serving them. All the reward that Satan will give them for the service which they do him, is to devour them. — I proceed now.

IV. To give the reasons of the doctrine, which I would do in answer to these two inquires. First, why God requires prayer in order to the bestowment of mercies, and secondly, why God is so ready to hear prayers of men?

INQ. I. Why does God require prayer in order to the bestowment of mercies?

It is not in order that God may be informed of our wants or desires. He is omniscient, and with respect to his knowledge, unchangeable. God never gains any knowledge by information. He knows what we want a thousand times more perfectly than we do ourselves, before we ask him. For though, speaking after the manner of men, God is sometimes represented as if he were moved and persuaded by the prayers of his people. Yet it is not to be thought that God is properly moved or made willing by our prayers. For it is no more possible that there should be any new inclination or will in God than new knowledge...It is the will of God to bestow mercy in this way, viz. in answer to prayer, when he designs beforehand to bestow mercy, yea, when he has promised it, as Eze. 36:35, 37, "I the Lord have spoken it, and will do it. Thus saith the Lord, I will yet for this be inquired of by the house of Israel, to do it for them." God has been pleased to constitute prayer, to be antecedent to the bestowment of mercy. And he is pleased to bestow mercy in consequence of prayer, as though he were prevailed on by prayer. — When the people of God are stirred up to prayer, it is the effect of his intention to show mercy. Therefore, he pours out the spirit of grace and supplication.

There may be two reasons given why God requires prayer in order to the bestowment of mercy: one especially respects God, and the other respects ourselves.

First, with respect to *God*, prayer is but a sensible acknowledgment of our dependence on him to his glory. As he has made all things for his own glory, so he will be glorified and acknowledged by his creatures. And it is fit that he should require this of those who would be the subjects of his mercy, that we, when we desire to receive any mercy from him, should humbly supplicate the Divine Being. For the bestowment of that mercy, is but a suitable acknowledgment of our dependence on the power and mercy of God for that which we need, and but a suitable honor paid to the great Author and Fountain of all good.

Second, with respect to *ourselves*, God requires prayer of us in order to the bestowment of mercy, because it tends to prepare us for its reception. Fervent prayer many ways tends to prepare the heart. Hereby is excited a sense of our need, and of the value of the mercy which we seek, and at the same times earnest desires for it, whereby the mind is more prepared to prize it, to rejoice in it when bestowed, and to be thankful for it. Prayer, with suitable confession, may excite a sense of our unworthiness of the mercy we seek. And the placing of ourselves in the immediate presence of God, may make us sensible of his majesty, and in a sense fit to receive mercy of him. Our prayer to God may excite in us a suitable sense and consideration of our dependence on God for the mercy we ask, and a suitable exercise of faith in God's sufficiency, that so we may be prepared to glorify his name when the mercy is received.

INQ. II. Why is God so ready to hear the prayers of men? — To this I answer,

First, because he is a God of infinite grace and mercy. It is indeed a very wonderful thing, that so great a God should be so ready to hear our prayers, though we are so despicable and unworthy. That he should give free access at all times to everyone, should allow us to be importunate without esteeming it an indecent boldness, [and] should be so rich in mercy to them that call upon him: that worms of the dust should have such power with God by prayer, that he should do such great things in answer to their prayers, and should show himself, as it were, overcome by them. This is very wonderful, when we consider the distance between God and us, and how we have provoked him by our sins, and how unworthy we are of the least gracious notice. It cannot be from any need that God stands in of us, for our goodness extends not to him. Neither can it be from anything in us to incline the heart of God to us. It cannot be from any worthiness in our prayers, which are in themselves polluted things. But it is because God delights in mercy and condescension. He is herein infinitely distinguished from all other gods. He is the great fountain of all good, from whom goodness flows as light from the sun.

Second, we have a glorious Mediator, who has prepared the way, that our prayers may be heard consistently with the honor of God's justice and majesty. Not only has God in himself mercy sufficient for this, but the Mediator has provided that this mercy may be exercised consistently with the divine honor. Through him we may come to God for mercy. He is the way, the truth, and the life. No man can come to the Father but by him. This Mediator hath done three things to make way for the hearing of our prayers.

1. He hath by his blood made *atonement* for sin, so that our guilt need not stand in the way, as a separating wall between God and us, and that our sins might not be a cloud through which our prayers cannot pass. By his atonement he hath made the way to the throne of grace open. God would have been infinitely gracious if there had been no Mediator, but the way to the mercy-seat would have been blocked up. But Christ hath removed whatever stood in the way. The veil which was before the mercy-seat "is rent from the top to the bottom" by the death of Christ. If it had not been for this, our guilt would have remained as a wall of brass to hinder our approach. But all is removed by his blood, Heb. 10:17, etc.

2. Christ, by his obedience, has *purchased* this privilege, viz. that the prayers of those who believe in him should be heard. He has not only removed the obstacles to our prayers, but has merited a hearing of them. His merits are the incense that is offered with the prayers of the saints, which renders them a sweet savor to God, and acceptable in his sight. Hence the prayers of the saints have such power with God. Hence at the prayer of a poor worm of the dust, God stopped the sun in his course for about the space of a whole day. Hence Jacob as a prince had power with God, and prevailed. Our prayers would be of no account, and of no avail with God, were

it not for the merits of Christ.

3. Christ enforces the prayers of his people, by his *intercession* at the right hand of God in heaven. He hath entered for us into the holy of holies, with the incense which he hath provided, and there he makes continual intercession for all that come to God in his name, so that their prayers come to God the Father through his hands, if I may so say, which is represented in Rev. 8:3, 4, "And another angel came and stood at the altar, having a golden censer; and there was given unto him much incense, that he should offer it with the prayers of all the saints upon the golden altar, which is before the throne. And the smoke of the incense which came with the prayers of the saints, ascended up before God, out of the angel's hand." — This was typified of old by the priest's offering incense in the temple, at the time when the people were offering up their prayers to God, as Luke 1:10, "And the whole multitude of the people were praying without at the time of incense."

APPLICATION

Hence we may learn how highly we are privileged, in that we have the Most High revealed to us, who is a God that heareth prayer. The greater part of mankind are destitute of this privilege. Whatever their necessities are, whatever their calamities or sorrows, they have no prayer-hearing God to whom they may go. If they go to the gods whom they worship, and cry to them ever so earnestly, it will be in vain. They worship either lifeless things that can neither help them nor know that they need help, or wicked cruel spirits, who are their enemies, and wish nothing but their misery, and who, instead of helping them, are from day to day working their ruin and watching over them as a hungry lion watches over his prey.

How are we distinguished from them, in that we have the true God made known to us: a God of infinite grace and mercy, a God full of compassion to the miserable, who is ready to pity us under all our troubles and sorrows, to hear our cries, and to give us all the relief which we need, a God who delights in mercy and is rich unto all that call upon him! How highly privileged are we, in that we have the holy Word of this same God, to direct us how to seek for mercy! And whatever difficulties or distress we are in, we may go to him with confidence and great encouragement. What a comfort may this be to us! And what reason have we to rejoice in our privileges, to prize them so highly, and to bless God that he hath been so merciful to us, as to give us his Word, and reveal himself to us; and that he hath not left us to cry for help to stocks and stones, and devils, as he has left many thousands of others.

OBJECTION. I have often prayed to God for certain mercies, and he has not heard my prayers. — To this I answer,

I. It is no argument, that God is not a prayer-hearing God, if he give not to men *what they ask* of him to consume upon their lusts. Oftentimes when men pray for temporal good things, they desire them for no good end, but only to gratify their pride or sensuality. If they pray for worldly good things chiefly from a worldly spirit and make an idol of the world, it is no wonder that God doth not hear their prayers. Jam. 4:3, "Ye ask, and receive not, because ye ask amiss, to consume it upon your lusts." If you request him to give you something of which you will make an idol, and set up in opposition to him — or will use as weapons of warfare against him, or as instruments to serve his enemies — no wonder that God will not hear you. If God should hear such prayers, he would act as his own enemy, inasmuch as he would bestow them to serve his enemies.

II. It is no argument that God is not a prayer-hearing God, that he heareth not *insincere* and *unbelieving* prayers. How can we expect that he should have any respect to that which has no sincerity in it? God looketh not at words, but at the heart; and it is fit that he should do so. If men pray only in words, and not in heart, what are their prayers good for? And why should that God who searches the heart, and tries the reins, have any respect of them? — Sometimes men do nothing but dissemble in their prayers. And when they do so, it is no argument that God is the less a prayer-hearing God, that he doth not hear such prayers, for it is no argument of want of mercy. Sometimes they pray for that in words which they really desire not in their hearts, as that he would purge them from sin, when at the same time they show by their practice, that they do not desire to be purged from sin, while they love and choose it and are utterly averse to parting with it. In like manner, they often dissemble in the pretense and show, which they make in their prayers, of dependence on God for mercies, and of a sense of his sufficiency to supply them. In our coming to God, and praying to him for such and such things, there is a show that we are sensible we are dependent on him for them, and that he is sufficient to give them to us. But men sometimes seem to pray, while not sensible of their dependence on God, nor do they think him sufficient to supply them. For all the while they trust in themselves, and have no confidence in God. — They show in words as though they were beggars, but in heart they come as creditors, and look on God as their debtor. In words they seem to ask for things as the fruit of free grace. But in heart they account it would be hard, unjust, and cruel, if God should deny them. In words they seem humble and submissive, but in heart they are proud and contentious. There is no prayer but in their words.

It doth not render God at all the less a prayer-hearing God, that he distinguishes, as an all-seeing God, between real prayers and pretend ones. Such prayers as those which I have just now been mentioning, are not worthy of the name in the eyes of him who searches the heart and sees things as they are. — That prayer which is not *of faith* is insincere, for prayer is a show or manifestation of dependence on God and trust in his sufficiency and mercy. Therefore, where this trust or *faith* is wanting, there is no prayer in the sight of God. And however God is sometimes pleased to grant the requests of those who have no faith, yet he has not obliged himself so to do. Nor is it an argument of his not being a prayer-hearing God, when he hears them not.

III. It is no argument that he is not a prayer-hearing God, that he exercises *his own wisdom* as to the time and manner of answering prayer. Some of God's people are sometimes ready to think that he does not hear their prayers, because he does [not] answer them at times when they expected, when indeed God hears them, and will answer them, in the time and way to which his own wisdom directs. — The business of prayer is not to direct God, who is infinitely wise and needs not any of our direction, who knows what is best for us ten thousand times better that we, and knows what time and what way are best. It is fit that he should answer prayer, and as an infinitely wise God in the exercise of his own wisdom, and not ours. God will deal as a father with us, in answering our requests. But a child is not to expect that the father's wisdom be subject to his, nor ought he to desire it, but should esteem it a privilege, that the parent will provide for him according to his *own* wisdom.

As to particular temporal blessings for which we pray, it is no argument that he is not a prayer-hearing God, because he bestows them not upon us. For it may be that God sees the things for which we pray not to be best for us. If so, it would be no mercy in him to bestow them upon us, but a judgment. Such things, therefore, ought always to be asked with submission to the divine will. God can answer prayer, though he bestow not the very thing for which we pray. He can sometimes better answer the lawful desires and good end we have in prayer another way. If our end be our own good and happiness, God can perhaps better answer that end in bestowing something else than in the bestowment of that very thing which we ask and if the main good we aim at in our prayer be attained, our prayer is answered, though not in the bestowment of the individual thing which we sought. And so that may still be true which was before asserted, *that God always hears the prayer* OF FAITH. God never once failed of hearing a *sincere* and *believing* prayer; and those promises forever hold good, "Ask, and ye shall receive; seek, and ye shall find; knock, and it shall be opened to you: for every one that asketh, receiveth; and he that seeketh, findeth; and to him that knocketh, it shall be opened."

Another use of this doctrine may be of reproof to those that neglect the duty of prayer. If we enjoy so great a privilege as to have the prayer-hearing God revealed to us, how great will be our folly and inexcusableness if we neglect the privilege, or make no use of it, and deprive ourselves of the advantage by not seeking this God by prayer. They are hereby reproved who neglect the great duty of secret prayer, which is more expressly required in the Word of God than any other kind. What account can those persons give of themselves, who neglect so known a duty? It is impossible that any among us should be ignorant of this command of God. How daring, therefore, is their wickedness who live in the neglect of this duty! And what can they answer to their Judge, when he shall call them to an account for it?

Here I shall briefly say something to an EXCUSE which some may be ready to make for themselves. Some may be ready to say *If I do pray, my prayer will not be the prayer of faith, because I am in a natural condition, and have no faith.*

This excuses not from obedience to a plain command of God. The command is to all to whom the command shall come. God not only directs godly persons to pray, but others also. In the beginning of the second chapter of Proverbs, God directs all persons to cry after wisdom and to lift up their voices for understanding, in order to their obtaining the fear and knowledge of God. And in Jam. 1:5, the apostle says, "If any man lack wisdom, let him ask of God." And Peter directed *Simon Magus* to repent and pray to God, if perhaps the thought of his heart might be forgiven him, Acts 8:22. Therefore when God says, do thus or thus, it is not for us to make excuses, but we must do the thing required. Besides, God is pleased sometimes to answer the prayers of unbelievers. Indeed he hears not their prayers for their goodness or acceptableness, or because of any true respect to him manifested in them, for there is none. Nor has he obliged himself to answer such prayers. Yet he is pleased sometimes, of his sovereign mercy, to pity wicked men, and hear their cries. Thus he heard the cries of the Ninevites (Jonah 3) and the prayer of Ahab, 1 Kin. 21:27, 28. Though there be no regard to God in their prayers yet he, of his infinite grace, is pleased to have respect to their desires of their own happiness, and to grant their requests. He may, and sometimes does, hear the cries of wicked men, as he hears the hungry ravens when they cry, Psa. 147:9. And as he opens his bountiful hand and satisfies the desires of every living thing, Psa. 145:16. Besides the prayers of sinners, though they have no goodness in them, yet are made a means of a preparation for mercy.

Finally, seeing we have such a prayer-hearing God as we have heard, let us be much employed in the duty of prayer. Let us pray with all prayer and supplication. Let us live prayerful lives, continuing instant in prayer, watching thereunto with all perseverance. Praying always, without ceasing, earnestly, and not fainting.

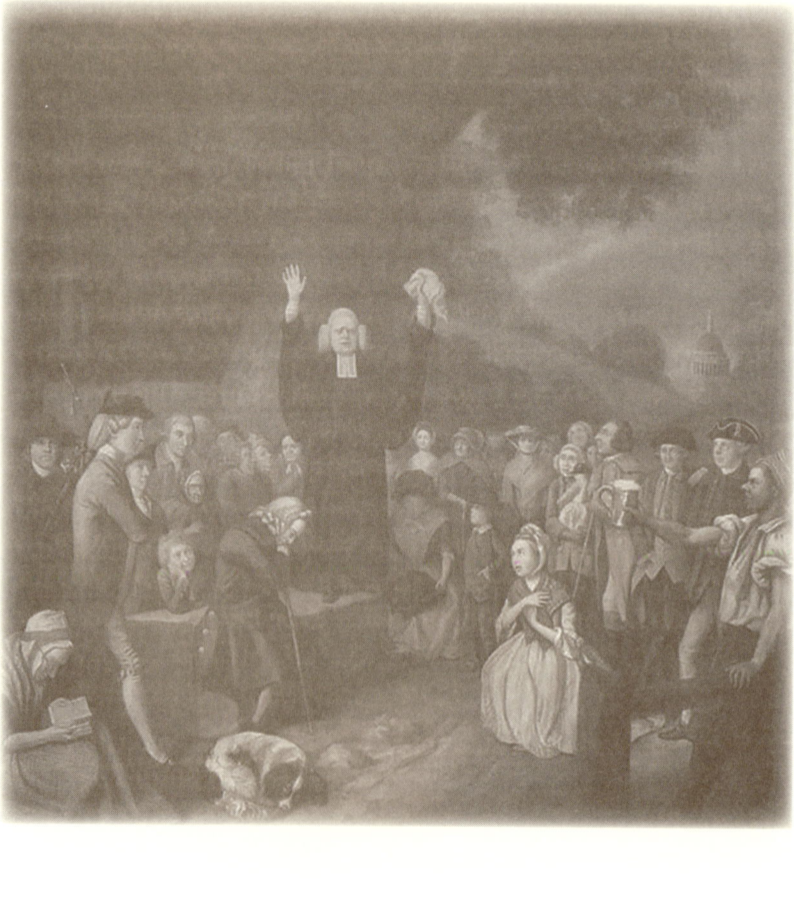

George Whitefield's Sermon on Prayer

Intercession, Every Christian's Duty

1 Thessalonians 5:25,
"Brethren, pray for us."

Sermon

If we inquire, why there is so little love to be found amongst Christians, why the very characteristic, by which every one should know that we are disciples of the holy Jesus, is almost banished out of the Christian world, we shall find it, in a great measure, owing to a neglect or superficial performance of that excellent part of prayer, INTERCESSION, or imploring the divine grace and mercy in behalf of others. Some forget this duty of praying for others, because they seldom remember to pray for themselves: and even those who are constant in praying to their Father who is in heaven, are often so selfish in their addresses to the throne of grace, that they do not enlarge their petitions for the welfare of their fellow Christians as they ought; and thereby fall short of attaining that Christian charity, that unfeigned love to their brethren, which their sacred profession obliges them to aspire after, and without which, though they should bestow all their goods to feed the poor, and even give their bodies to be burned, yet it would profit them nothing. Since these things are so, I shall from the words of the text (though originally intended to be more confined) endeavor, to show,

I. FIRST, That it is every Christian's duty to pray for others as well as for himself.

II. SECONDLY, Show, whom we ought to pray for, and in what manner we should do it. And,

III. THIRDLY, I shall offer some motives to excite all Christians to abound in this great duty of intercession.

I. FIRST, I shall endeavor to show, That it is every Christian's duty to pray for others, as well as for himself.

Now PRAYER is a duty founded on natural religion; the very heathens never neglected it, though many Christian heathens amongst us do: and it is so essential to Christianity, that you might as reasonably expect to find a living man without breath, as a true Christian without the spirit of prayer and supplication. Thus, no sooner was St. Paul converted, but "behold he prayeth," saith the Lord Almighty. And thus will it be with every child of God, as soon as he becomes such: prayer being truly called, The natural cry of the new-born soul. For in the heart of every true believer there is a heavenly tendency, a divine attraction, which as sensibly draws him to converse with God, as the lodestone attracts the needle. A deep sense of their own weakness, and of Christ's fullness; a strong conviction of their natural corruption, and of the necessity of renewing grace; will not let them rest from crying day and night to their Almighty Redeemer, that the divine image, which they lost in Adam, may through his all-powerful mediation, and the sanctifying operation of his blessed spirit, be begun, carried on, and fully perfected both in their souls and bodies.

Thus earnest, thus importunate, are all sincere Christians in praying for themselves: but then, not having so lively, lasting, and deep a sense of the wants of their Christian brethren, they are for the most part too remiss and defective in their prayers for them. Whereas, was the love of God shed abroad in our hearts, and did we love our neighbor in that manner, in which the Son of God our savior loved us, and according to his command and example, we could not but be as importunate for their spiritual and temporal welfare, as for our own; and as earnestly desire and endeavor that others should share in the benefits of the death and passion of Jesus Christ, as we ourselves.

Let not any one think, that this is an uncommon degree of charity; an high pitch of perfection, to which not every one can attain: for, if we are all commanded to "love our neighbor (that is every man) even as ourselves," nay to "lay down our lives for the brethren;" then, it is the duty of all to pray for their neighbors as much as for themselves, and by all possible acts and expressions of love and affection towards them, at all times, to show their readiness even to lay down their lives for them, if ever it should please God to call them to it.

Our blessed Savior, as "he hath set us an example, that we should follow his steps" in every thing else, so hath he more especially in this: for in that divine, that perfect and inimitable prayer (recorded in the 17th of St. John) which he put up just before his passion, we find but few petitions for his own, though many for his disciples welfare: and in that perfect form which he has been pleased to prescribe us, we are taught to say, not MY, but "OUR Father," thereby to put us in mind, that, whenever we approach the throne of grace, we ought to pray not for ourselves alone, but for all our brethren in Christ. Intercession then is certainly a duty incumbent upon all Christians.

II. Whom we are to intercede for, and how this duty is to be performed, comes next to be considered.

1. And first, our intercession must be UNIVERSAL. "I will, (says the apostle) that prayers, supplications and intercessions be made for all men." For as God's mercy is over all his works, as Jesus Christ died to redeem a people out of all nations and languages; so we should pray, that "all men may come to the knowledge of the truth, and be saved." Many precious promises are made in holy writ, that the gospel shall be published through the whole world, that "the earth shall be covered with the knowledge of the Lord, as the waters cover the sea:" and therefore it is our duty not to confine our petitions to our own nation, but to pray that all those nations, who now sit in darkness and in the shadow of death, may have the glorious gospel shine out upon them, as well as upon us. But you need not that any man should teach you this, since ye yourselves are taught of God, and of Jesus Christ himself, to pray, that his kingdom may come; part of the meaning of which petition is, that "God's ways may be known upon earth, and his saving health among all nations."

2. Next to the praying for all men, we should, according to St. Paul's rule, pray for KINGS; particularly for our present sovereign King George, and all that are put in authority under him: that we may lead quiet lives, in all godliness and honesty. For, if we consider how heavy the burden of government is, and how much the welfare of any people depends on the zeal and godly conversation of those that have the rule over them: if we set before us the many dangers and difficulties, to which governors by their station are exposed, and the continual temptations they be under to luxury and self-indulgence; we shall not only pity, but pray for them: that he who preserved Esther, David, and Josiah, "unspotted from the world," amidst the grandeur of a court, and gave success to their designs, would also preserve them holy and unblameable, and prosper all the works of their hands upon them. But

3. THIRDLY, you ought, in a more especial manner, to pray for those, whom "the Holy Ghost hath made OVERSEERS over you." This is what St. Paul begs, again and again, of the churches to whom he writes: Says he in the text, "Brethren, pray for us;" and again, in his epistle to the Ephesians, "praying always, with all manner of supplication; and for me also, that I may open my mouth boldly, to declare the mystery of the gospel." And in another place, to express his earnestness in this request, and the great importance of their prayers for him, he bids the church "strive, (or, as the original word signifies, be in a agony) together with him in their prayers." And surely, if the great St. Paul, that chosen vessel, that favorite of heaven, needed the most

importunate prayers of his Christian converts; much more do the ordinary ministers of the gospel stand in need of the intercession of their respective flocks. And I cannot but in a more especial manner insist upon this branch of your duty, because it is a matter of such importance: for, no doubt, much good is frequently withheld from many, by reason of their neglecting to pray for their ministers, and which they would have received, had they prayed for them as they ought. Not to mention, that people often complain of the want of diligent and faithful pastors. But how do they deserve good pastors, who will not earnestly pray to God for such? If we will not pray to the Lord of the harvest, can it be expected he will send forth laborers into his harvest?

Besides, what ingratitude is it, not to pray for your ministers! For shall they watch and labor in the word and doctrine for you, and your salvation, and shall not you pray for them in return? If any bestow favors on your bodies, you think it right, meet, and your bounden duty, to pray for them; and shall not they be remembered in your prayers, who daily feed and nourish your souls? Add to all this, that praying for your ministers, will be a manifest proof of your believing, that though Paul plant, and Apollos water, yet it is God alone who giveth the increase. And you will also find it the best means you can use, to promote your own welfare; because God, in answer to your prayers, may impart a double portion of his Holy Spirit to them, whereby they will be qualified to deal out to you larger measures of knowledge in spiritual things, and be enabled more skillfully to divide the word of truth.
Would men but constantly observe this direction, and when their ministers are praying in their name to God, humbly beseech him to perform all their petitions: or, when they are speaking in God's name to them, pray that the Holy Ghost may fall on all them that hear the word; we should find a more visible good effect of their doctrine, and a greater mutual love between ministers and their people. For ministers hands would then be hold up by the people's intercessions, and the people will never dare to villify or traduce those who are the constant subjects of their prayers.

4. Next to our ministers, OUR FRIENDS claim a place in our intercessions; but then we should not content ourselves with praying in general terms for them, but suit our prayers to their particular circumstances. When Miriam was afflicted with a leprosy from God, Moses cried and said, "Lord, heal her." And when the nobleman came to apply to Jesus Christ, in behalf of his child, he said, "Lord, my little daughter lieth at the point of death, I pray thee to come and heal her." In like manner, when our friends are under any afflicting circumstances, we should endeavor to pray for them, with a particular regard to those circumstances.

For instance, is a friend sick? We should pray, that if it be God's good pleasure, it may not be unto death; but is otherwise, that he would give him grace so to take his visitation, that, after this painful life ended, he may dwell with him in life everlasting. Is a friend in doubt in an important matter? We should lay his case before God, as Moses did that of the daughters of Zelophehad, and pray, that God's Holy Spirit may lead him into all truth, and give all seasonable direction. Is he in want? We should pray, that his faith may never fail, and that in God's due time he may be relieved. And in all other cases, we should not pray for our friends only in generals, but suit our petitions to their particular sufferings and afflictions; for otherwise, we may never ask perhaps for the things our friends most want.

It must be confessed, that such a procedure will oblige some often to break from the forms they use; but if we accustom ourselves to it, and have a deep sense of what we ask for, the most illiterate will want proper words to express themselves.

We have many noble instances in holy scripture of the success of this kind of particular intercession; but none more remarkable than that of Abraham's servant, in the book of Genesis, who being sent to seek a wife for his son Isaac, prayed in a most particular manner in his behalf. And the sequel of the story informs us, how remarkably his prayer was answered. And did Christians now pray for their friends in the same particular manner, and with the same faith as Abraham's servant did for his master; they would, no doubt, in many instances, receive as visible answers, and have as much reason to bless God for them, as he had. But

5. As we ought thus to intercede for our friends, so in like manner must we also pray for OUR ENEMIES. "Bless them that curse you, (says Jesus Christ) and pray for them that despitefully use you, and persecute you." Which commands he enforced in the strongest manner by his own example: in the very agonies and pangs of death, he prayed even for his murderers, "Father, forgive them, for they know not what they do!" This, it must needs be confessed, is a difficult duty, yet not impracticable, to those who have renounced the things of this present life, (from an inordinate love of which all enmities arise) and who knowing the terrible woes denounced against those who offend Christ's little ones, can, out of real pity, and a sense of their danger, pray for those by whom such offenses come.

6. Lastly, and to conclude this head, we should intercede for all that are any ways AFFLICTED in mind, body, or estate; for all who desire, and stand in need of our prayers, and for all who do not pray for themselves.

And Oh! That all who hear me, would set apart some time every day for the due performance of this most necessary duty! In order to which, I shall now proceed,

III. To show the advantages, and offer some considerations to excite you to the practice of daily intercession. And

1. FIRST, It will fill your hearts with love one to another. He that every day heartily intercedes at the throne of grace for all mankind, cannot but in a short time be filled with love and charity to all: and the frequent exercise of his love in this manner, will insensibly enlarge his heart, and make him partaker of that exceeding abundance of it which is in Christ Jesus our Lord! Envy, malice, revenge, and such like hellish tempers, can never long harbor in a gracious intercessor's breast; but he will be filled with joy, peace, meekness, long-suffering, and all other graces of the Holy Spirit. By frequently laying his neighbor's wants before God, he will be touched with a fellow-feeling of them; he will rejoice with those that do rejoice, and weep with those that weep. Every blessing bestowed on others, instead of exciting envy in him, will be looked on as an answer to his particular intercession, and fill his soul with joy unspeakable and full of glory.

Abound therefore in acts of general and particular intercessions; and when you hear of your neighbor's faults, instead of relating them to, and exposing them before others, lay them in secret before God, and beg of him to correct and amend them. When you hear of a notorious sinner, instead of thinking you do well to be angry, beg of Jesus Christ to convert, and make him a monument of his free grace; you cannot imagine what a blessed alteration this practice will make in your heart, and how much you will increase day by day in the spirit of love and meekness towards all mankind! But farther, to excite you to the constant practice of this duty of intercession, consider the many instances in holy scripture, of the power and efficacy of it. Great and excellent things are there recorded as the effects of this divine employ. It has stopped plagues, it has opened and shut heaven; and has frequently turned away God's fury from his people. How was Abimelech's house freed from the disease God sent amongst them, at the intercession of Abraham! When "Phineas stood up and prayed," how soon did the plague cease! When Daniel humbled and afflicted his soul, and interceded for the Lord's inheritance, how quickly was an angel dispatched to tell him, "his prayer was heard!" And, to mention but one instance more, how does God own himself as it were overcome with the importunity of Moses, when he was interceding for his idolatrous people, "Let me alone," says God!

This sufficiently shows, I could almost say, the omnipotency of intercession, and how we may, like Jacob, wrestle with God, and by an holy violence prevail both for ourselves and others. And no doubt it is owing to the secret and prevailing intercessions of the few righteous souls who still remain among us, that God has yet spared this miserably sinful nation: for were there not some such faithful ones, like Moses, left to stand in the gap, we should soon be destroyed, even as was Sodom, and reduced to ashes like unto Gomorrah.

But, to stir you up yet farther to this exercise of intercession, consider, that in all probability, it is the frequent employment even of the glorified saints: for though they are delivered from the burden of the flesh, and restored to the glorious liberty of the sons of God, yet as their happiness cannot be perfectly consummated till the resurrection of the last day, when all their brethren will be glorified with them...And shall now we, who are on earth, be often exercised in this divine employ with the glorious company of the spirits of just men made perfect? Since our happiness is so much to consist in the communion of saints in the church triumphant above, shall we not frequently intercede for the church militant here below; and earnestly beg, that we may all be one, even as the Holy Jesus and his Father are one, that we may also be made perfect in one?

To provoke you to this great work and labor of love, remember, that it is the never ceasing employment of the holy and highly exalted Jesus himself, who sits at the right hand of God, to hear all our prayers, and to make continual intercession for us! So that he who is constantly employed in interceding for others, is doing that on earth, which the eternal Son of God is always doing in heaven.

Imagine therefore, when you are lifting up holy hands in prayer for one another, that you see the heavens opened, and the Son of God in all his glory, as the great high-priest of your salvation, pleading for you the all-sufficient merit of his sacrifice before the throne of his heavenly Father! Join then your intercessions with his, and beseech him, that they may, through him, come up as incense, and be received as a sweet-smelling savor, acceptable in the sight of God! This imagination will strengthen your faith, excite a holy earnestness in your prayers, and make you wrestle with God, as Jacob did, when he saw him face to face, and his life was preserved; as Abraham, when he pleaded for Sodom; and as Jesus Christ himself, when he prayed, being in an agony, so much the more earnestly the night before his bitter passion.

And now, brethren, what shall I say more, since you are taught of Jesus Christ himself, to abound in love, and in this good work of praying one for another. Though ever so mean, though as poor as Lazarus, you will then become benefactors to all mankind; thousands, and twenty times ten thousands, will then be blessed for your sakes! And after you have employed a few years in this divine exercise here, you will be translated to that happy place, where you have so often wished others might be advanced; and be exalted to sit at the right hand of our All-powerful, All-prevailing Intercessor, in the kingdom of his heavenly Father hereafter.

However, I cannot but in an especial manner press this upon you now, because all ye, amongst whom I have now been preaching, in all probability will see me no more: for I am now going (I trust under the conduct of God's most Holy Spirit) from you, knowing not what shall befall me: I need therefore your most importunate intercessions, that nothing may move me from my duty, and that I may not "count even my life dear unto myself, so that I may finish my course with joy, and the ministry I have received of the Lord Jesus, to testify the gospel of the grace of God!"

Whilst I have been here, to the best of my knowledge, I have not failed to declare unto you the whole will of God: and though my preaching may have been a savor of death unto death to some; yet I trust it has been also a savor of life unto life to others; and therefore I earnestly hope that those will not fail to remember me in their prayers. As for my own part, the many unmerited kindnesses I have received from you, will not suffer me to forget you: out of the deep, therefore, I trust shall my cry come unto God; and whilst the winds and storms are blowing over me, unto the Lord will I make my supplication for you. For it is but a little while, and "we must all appear before the judgment seat of Christ;" where I must give a strict account of the doctrine I have preached, and you of your improvement under it. And O that I may never be called out as a swift witness, against any of those, for whose salvation I have sincerely, though too faintly, longed and labored!

It is true, I have been censured by some as acting out of sinister and selfish views; "but it is a small matter with me to be judged by man's judgment; I hope my eye is single; but I beseech you, brethren, by the mercies of God in Christ Jesus, pray that it may be more so! And that I may increase with the increase of grace in the knowledge and love of God through Jesus Christ our Lord.

And now, brethren, what shall I say more? I could wish to continue my discourse much longer; for I can never fully express the desire of my soul towards you! Finally, therefore, brethren, "whatsoever things are holy, whatsoever things are pure, whatsoever things are honest, whatsoever things are of good report: if there be any consolation in Christ, if any fellowship of the spirit," if any hopes of our appearing to the comfort of each other at the awful tribunal of Jesus Christ, "think of the things that you have heard," and of those which your pastors have declared, and will yet declare unto you; and continue under their ministry to "work out your own salvation with fear and trembling:" so that whether I should never see you any more, or whether it shall please God to bring me back again at any time, I may always have the satisfaction of knowing that your conversation is such "as becometh the gospel of Christ."

I almost persuade myself, that I could willingly suffer all things, so that it might any ways promote the salvation of your precious and immortal souls; and I beseech you, as my last request, "obey them that have the rule over you in the Lord;" and be always ready to attend on their ministry, as it is your bounden duty. Think not that I desire to have myself exalted at the expense of another's character; but rather think this, not to have any man's person too much in admiration; but esteem all your ministers highly in love, as they justly deserve for their work's sake.

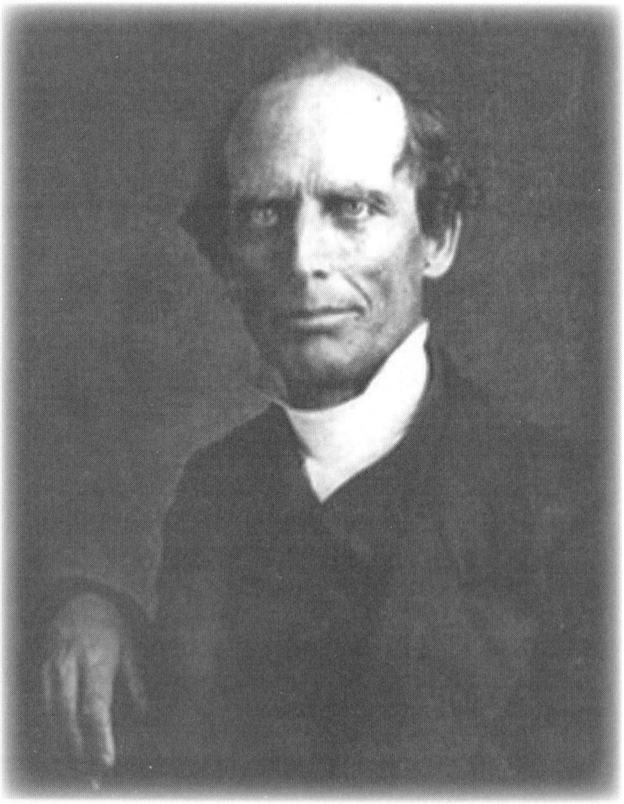

Charles G. Finney's Sermon on Prayer

Prevailing Prayer

TEXT. --*The effectual, fervent prayer of a righteous man availeth much.--*
JAMES 5:16

THE last lecture referred principally to the confession of sin. To-night my remarks will be chiefly confined to the subject of intercession, or prayer. There are two kinds of means requisite to promote a revival; one to influence men, the other to influence God. The truth is employed to influence men, and prayer to move God. When I speak of moving God, I do not mean that God's mind is changed by prayer, or that his disposition or character is changed. But prayer produces such a change in us and fulfills such conditions as renders it consistent for God to do as it would not be consistent for him to do otherwise. When a sinner repents, that state of mind makes it proper for God to forgive him. God has always been ready to forgive him on that condition, so that when the sinner changes his mind towards God, it requires no change of feeling in God to pardon him. It is the sinner's repentance that renders his forgiveness proper, and is the occasion of God's acting as he does. So when Christians offer effectual prayer, their state of mind renders it proper for God to answer them. He was always ready to bestow the blessing, on the condition that they felt right, and offered the right kind of prayer. Whenever this change takes place in them, and they offer the right kind of prayer, then God, without any change in himself, can answer them. When we offer effectual fervent prayer for others, the fact that we offer such prayer renders it consistent for him to do what we pray for, when otherwise it would not have been consistent.

Prayer is an essential link in the chain of causes that lead to a revival; as much so as truth is. Some have zealously used truth to convert men, and laid very little stress on prayer. They have preached, and talked, and distributed tracts with great zeal, and then wondered that they had so little success. And the reason was, that they forgot to use the other branch of the means, effectual prayer. They overlooked the fact, that truth by itself will never produce the effect, without the Spirit of God, and that Spirit is given in answer to earnest prayer.

Sometimes it happens that those who are the most engaged in employing truth, are not the most engaged in prayer. This is always unhappy.--For unless they, or somebody else have the spirit of prayer, the truth by itself will do nothing but harden men in impenitence. Probably in the day of judgment it will be found that nothing is ever done by the truth, used ever so zealously, unless there is a spirit of prayer somewhere in connection with the presentation of truth.

Others err on the other side. Not that they lay too much stress on prayer. But they overlook the fact that prayer might be offered for ever, by itself, and nothing would be done. Because sinners are not converted by direct contact of the Holy Ghost, but by the truth, employed as a means. To expect the conversion of sinners by prayer alone, without the employment of truth, is to tempt God.

The subject of discourse this evening, is

PREVAILING PRAYER.

I. I propose to show what is effectual or prevailing prayer.
II. State some of the most essential attributes of prevailing prayer.
III. Give some reasons why God requires this kind of prayer.
IV. Show that such prayer will avail much.

I. I proceed to show what is prevailing prayer.

1. Effectual, prevailing prayer, does not consist in benevolent desires merely. Benevolent desires are doubtless pleasing to God. Such desires pervade heaven, and are found in all holy beings. But they are not prayer. Men may have these desires as the angels and glorified spirits have them. But this is not the effectual, prevailing prayer, spoken of in the text. Prevailing prayer is something more than this.

2. Prevailing, or effectual prayer, is that prayer which obtains the blessing that it seeks. It is that prayer which effectually moves God. The very idea of effectual prayer is, that it effects its object.

II. I will state some of the most essential attributes of prevailing prayer.
I cannot detail in full all the things that go to make up prevailing prayer. But I will mention some things that are essential to it; some things which a person must do in order to prevail in prayer.

1. He must pray for a definite object. He need not expect to offer such prayer, if he prays at random, without any distinct or definite object. He

must have an object distinctly before his mind. I speak now of secret prayer. Many people go away into their closets, because they must say their prayers. The time has come that they are in the habit of going by themselves for prayer, in the morning, or at noon, or at whatever time of day it may be. And instead of having any thing to say, any definite object before their mind, they fall down on their knees, and pray for just what comes into their minds, for everything that floats in their imagination at the time, and when they have done, they could not tell hardly a word of what they have been praying for. This is not effectual prayer. What should we think of any body who should try to move a legislature so, and should say, "Now it is winter, and the legislature is in session, and it is time to send up petitions," and should go up to the legislature and petition at random, without any definite object? Do you think such petitions would move the legislature?

A man must have some definite object before his mind. He cannot pray effectually for a variety of objects at once. The mind of man is so constituted that it cannot fasten its desires intensely upon many things at the same time. All the instances of effectual prayer recorded in the Bible were of this kind. Wherever you see that the blessing sought for in prayer was attained, you will find that the prayer which was offered was prayer for that definite object.

2. Prayer, to be effectual, must be in accordance with the revealed will of God. To pray for things contrary to the revealed will of God, is to tempt God. There are three ways in which God's will is revealed to men for their guidance in prayer.

(1.) By express promises or predictions in the Bible, that he will give or do certain things. Either by express promises in regard to particular things, or promises in general terms, so that we may apply them to particular things. For instance, there is this promise: "Whatsoever things ye desire, when ye pray, believe that ye receive them, and ye shall have them."

(2.) Sometimes God reveals his will by his providence...God often makes it clear to those who have spiritual discernment...

(3.) By his Spirit. When God's people are at a loss what to pray for, agreeable to his will, his Spirit often instructs them. Where there is no particular revelation, and providence leaves it dark, and we know not what to pray for as we ought, we are expressly told, that "the Spirit also helpeth our infirmities," and "the Spirit itself maketh intercession for us with groanings that cannot be uttered"...It is just as plain here, as if it were now revealed by a voice from heaven, that the Spirit of God helps the people of God to pray according to the will of God, when they themselves know not what things they ought to pray for. "And he that searcheth the heart knoweth the mind of the Spirit," because he maketh intercession for the saints according to the will of God, and he leads Christians to pray for just those things, with groanings that cannot be uttered. When neither the word nor providence enables them to decide, then let them be filled with the Spirit, as God commands them to be. He says, "Be ye filled with the Spirit." And He will lead their mind to such things as God is willing to grant.

3. To pray effectually, you must pray with submission to the will of God. Do not confound submission with indifference. No two things are more unlike. I once knew an individual come where there was a revival. He himself was cold, and did not enter into the spirit of it, and had no spirit of prayer; and when he heard the brethren pray as if they could not be denied, he was shocked at their boldness, and kept all the time insisting on the importance of praying with submission; when it was as plain as anything could be, that he confounded submission with indifference.

So again, do not confound submission in prayer with a general confidence that God will do what is right. It is proper to have this confidence that God will do what is right in all things. But this is a different thing from submission. What I mean by submission in prayer, is, acquiescence in the revealed will of God. To submit to any command of God is to obey it. Submission to some supposable or possible, but secret decree of God, is not submission. To submit to any dispensation of Providence is impossible till it comes. For we never can know what the event is to be, till it takes place. Take a case: David, when his child was sick, was distressed, and agonized in prayer, and refused to be comforted. He took it so much to heart, that when the child died, his servants were afraid to tell him the child was dead, for fear he would vex himself still worse. But as soon as he heard that the child was dead, he laid aside his grief, and arose, and asked for food, and ate and drank as usual. While the child was yet alive, he did not know what was the will of God, and so he fasted and prayed, and said, "Who can tell whether God will be gracious to me, that my child may live?" He did not know but that his prayer and agony was the very thing on which it turned, whether the child was to live or not. He thought that if he humbled himself and entreated God, perhaps God would spare him this blow. But as soon as God's will appeared, and the child was dead, he bowed like a saint. He seemed not only to acquiesce, but actually to take a satisfaction in it. "I shall go to him, but he shall not return to me." This was true submission. He reasoned correctly in the case. While he had no revelation of the will of God, he did not know but what the child's recovery depended on his prayer. But when he had a revelation of the will of God, he submitted. While the will of God is not known, to submit, without prayer, is tempting God. Perhaps, and for aught you know, the fact of your offering the right kind of prayer, may be the thing on which the event turns. In the case of an impenitent friend, the very condition on which he is to be saved from hell, may be the fervency and importunity of your prayer for that individual.

4. Effectual prayer for an object implies a desire for that object commensurate with its importance. If a person truly desires any blessing, his desires will bear some proportion to the greatness of the blessing. The desires of the Lord Jesus Christ for the blessing he prayed for, were amazingly strong, and amounted even to agony. If the desire for an object is strong, and is a benevolent desire, and the thing not contrary to the will and providence of God, the presumption is, that it will be granted. There are two reasons for this presumption:

(1.) From the general benevolence of God. If it is a desirable object; if, so far as we can see, it would be an act of benevolence in God to grant it, his general benevolence is presumptive evidence that he will grant it.

(2.) If you find yourself exercised with benevolent desires for any object, there is a strong presumption that the Spirit of God is exciting these very desires, and stirring you up to pray for that object, so that it may be granted in answer to prayer. In such a case no degree of desire or importunity in prayer is improper. A Christian may come up, as it were, and take hold of the hand of God. See the case of Jacob, when he exclaimed, in an agony of desire, "I will not let thee go, except thou bless me." Was God displeased with his boldness and importunity? Not at all; but he granted him the very thing he prayed for. So in the case of Moses. God said to Moses, "Let me alone, that I may destroy them, and blot out their name from under heaven, and I will make of thee a nation mightier and greater than they." What did Moses do? Did he stand aside and let God do as he said? No, his mind runs back to the Egyptians, and he thinks how they will triumph. "Wherefore should the Egyptians say, For mischief did he bring them out." It seemed as if he took hold of the uplifted hand of God, to avert the blow. Did God rebuke him for his interference, and tell him he had no business to interfere? No; it seemed as if he was unable to deny any thing to such importunity, and so Moses stood in the gap, and prevailed with God.

It is said of Xavier, the missionary, that he was once called to pray for a man who was sick, and he prayed so fervently that he seemed as it were to do violence to heaven--so the writer expresses it. And he prevailed, and the man recovered.

Such prayer is often offered in the present day, when Christians have been wrought up to such a pitch of importunity and such a holy boldness, that afterwards, when they looked back upon it, they were frightened and amazed at themselves, to think they should dare to exercise such importunity with

God. And yet these prayers have prevailed, and obtained the blessing. And many of these persons, that I am acquainted with, are among the holiest persons I know in the world.

5. Prayer, to be effectual, must be offered from right motives. Prayer should not be selfish, but dictated by a supreme regard for the glory of God. A great deal of prayer is offered from pure selfishness. Women sometimes pray for their husbands, that they may be converted, because they say, "It would be so much more pleasant to have my husband go to meeting with me," and all that. And they seem never to lift up their thoughts above self at all. They do not seem to think how their husbands are dishonoring God by their sins, and how God would be glorified in their conversion. So it is with parents very often. They cannot bear to think that their children should be lost. They pray for them very earnestly indeed. But if you go to talk with them, they are very tender, and tell you how good their children are, how they respect religion, and they think they are almost Christians now; and so they talk as if they were afraid you would hurt their children if you should tell them the truth. They do not think how such amiable and lovely children are dishonoring God by their sins; they are only thinking what a dreadful thing it will be for them to go to hell. Ah! unless their thoughts rise higher than this, their prayers will never prevail with a holy God. The temptation to selfish motives is so strong, that there is reason to fear a great many parental prayers never rise above the yearnings of parental tenderness. And that is the reason why so many prayers are not heard, and why so many pious, praying parents have ungodly children. Much of the prayer for the heathen world seems to be based on no higher principle than sympathy. Missionary agents, and others, are dwelling almost exclusively upon the six hundred millions of heathens going to hell, while little is said of their dishonoring God. This is a great evil; and until the church have higher motives for prayer and missionary effort than sympathy for the heathen, their prayers and efforts will never amount to much.

6. Prayer, to be effectual, must be by the intercession of the Spirit. You never can expect to offer prayer according to the will of God without the Spirit. In the first two cases, it is not because Christians are unable to offer such prayer, where the will of God is revealed in his word, or indicated by his providence. They are able to do it, just as they are able to be holy. But the fact is, that they are so wicked, that they never do offer such prayer, without they are influenced by the Spirit of God. There must be a faith, such as produced by the effectual operation of the Holy Ghost.

7. It must be persevering prayer. As a general thing, Christians who have backslidden and lost the spirit of prayer, will not get at once into the habit of

persevering prayer. Their minds are not in a right state, and they cannot fix their minds, and hold on till the blessing comes. If their minds were in that state, that they would persevere till the answer comes, effectual prayer might be offered at once, as well as after praying ever so many times for an object. But they have to pray again and again, because their thoughts are so apt to wander away, and are so easily diverted from the object to something else. Until their minds get imbued with the spirit of prayer, they will not keep fixed to one point, and push their petition to an issue on the spot. Do not think you are prepared to offer prevailing prayer, if your feelings will let you pray once for an object, and then leave it. Most Christians come up to prevailing prayer by a protracted process. Their minds gradually become filled with anxiety about an object, so that they will even go about their business, sighing out their desires to God. Just as the mother whose child is sick, goes round her house, sighing as if her heart would break. And if she is a praying mother, her sighs are breathed out to God all the day long. If she goes out of the room where her child is, her mind is still on it; and if she is asleep, still her thoughts are on it, and she starts in her dreams, thinking it is dying. Her whole mind is absorbed in that sick child. This is the state of mind in which Christians offer prevailing prayer.

What was the reason that Jacob wrestled all night in prayer with God? He knew that he had done his brother Esau a great injury, in getting away the birthright a long time ago. And now he was informed that his injured brother was coming to meet him, with an armed force altogether too powerful for him to contend against. And there was great reason to suppose he was coming with a purpose of revenge. There were two reasons then why he should be distressed. The first was, that he had done this great injury, and had never made any reparation. The other was, that Esau was coming with a force sufficient to crush him. Now, what does he do? Why, he first arranges everything in the best manner he can to meet his brother, sending his present first, then his property, then his family, putting those he loved most farthest behind. And by this time his mind was so exercised that he could not contain himself. He goes away alone over the brook, and pours out his very soul in an agony of prayer all night. And just as the day was breaking, the angel of the covenant said, "Let me go;" and his whole being was, as it were, agonized at the thought of giving up, and he cried out, "I will not let thee go except thou bless me." His soul was wrought up into an agony, and he obtained the blessing, but he always bore the marks of it, and showed that his body had been greatly affected by this mental struggle. This is prevailing prayer.

Now, do not deceive yourselves with thinking that you offer effectual prayer, unless you have this intense desire for the blessing. I do not believe in it. Prayer is not effectual unless it is offered up with an agony of desire. The apostle Paul speaks of it as a travail of the soul. Jesus Christ, when he was praying in the garden, was in such an agony, that he sweat as it were great drops of blood falling down to the ground. I have never known a person sweat blood; but I have known a person pray till the blood started from the nose. And I have known persons pray till they were all wet with perspiration, in the coldest weather in winter. I have known persons pray for hours, till their strength was all exhausted with the agony of their minds. Such prayers prevailed with God.

This agony in prayer was prevalent in President Edwards' day, in the revivals that then took place. It was one of the great stumbling blocks in those days, to persons who were opposed to the revival, that people used to pray till their bodies were overpowered with their feelings. I will read a paragraph of what President Edwards says on the subject, to let you see that this is not a new thing in the Church, but has always prevailed wherever revivals prevailed with power. It is from his Thoughts on Revivals.

"We cannot determine that God never shall give any person so much of a discovery of himself, not only as to weaken their bodies, but to take away their lives. It is supposed by very learned and judicious divines, that Moses' life was taken away after this manner; and this has also been supposed to be the case with some other saints. Yea, I do not see any solid, sure grounds any have to determine, that God shall never make such strong impressions on the mind by his Spirit, that shall be an occasion of so impairing the frame of the body, and particularly that part of the body, the brain, that persons shall be deprived of the use of reason. As I said before, It is too much for us to determine, that God will not bring an outward calamity in bestowing spiritual and eternal blessings: so it is too much for us to determine, how great an outward calamity he will bring. If God give a great increase of discoveries of himself, and of love to him, the benefit is infinitely greater than the calamity, though the life should presently after be taken away; yea, though the soul should not immediately be taken to heaven, but should lie some years in a deep sleep, and then be taken to heaven; or, which is much the same thing, if it be deprived of the use of its faculties, and be inactive and unserviceable, as if it lay in a deep sleep for some years, and then should pass into glory. We cannot determine how great a calamity distraction is, when considered with all its consequences, and all that might have been consequent, if the distraction had not happened; nor indeed whether (thus considered) it be any calamity at all, or whether it be not a mercy, by preventing some great sin, or some more dreadful thing, if it had not been. It were a great fault in us to limit a sovereign, all-wise God, whose judgments are a great deep, and his ways past finding out, where he has not limited himself, and in things concerning which he has not told us what his way shall be. It is remarkable, considering in what multitudes of instances, and to how great a degree, the frame of the body has been overpowered of late, that persons' lives have, notwithstanding, been preserved, and that the instances of those that have been deprived of reason, have been so very few, and those, perhaps all of them, persons under the peculiar disadvantage of a weak, vapory habit of body. A merciful and careful Divine hand is very manifest in it, that in so many instances where the ship has begun to sink, yet it has been upheld, and has not totally sunk. The instances of such as have been deprived of reason are so few, that certainly they are not enough to cause us to be in any fright, as though this work that has been carried on in the country was like to be of baneful influence; unless we are disposed to gather up all that we can to darken it, and set it forth in frightful colors.

"There is one particular kind of exercise and concern of mind, that many have been overpowered by, that has been especially stumbling to some; and that is, the deep concern and distress that they have been in for the souls of others. I am sorry that any put us to the trouble of doing that which seems so needless, as defending such a thing as this. It seems like mere trifling, in so plain a case, to enter into a formal and particular debate, in order to determine whether there be anything in the greatness and importance of the case that will answer and bear a proportion to the greatness of the concern that some have manifested. Men may be allowed, from no higher a principle than common ingenuity and humanity, to be very deeply concerned and greatly exercised in mind at seeing others in great danger of no greater a calamity than drowning, or being burnt up in a house on fire. And if so, then doubtless it will be allowed to be equally reasonable, if they saw them in danger of a calamity ten times greater, to be still much more concerned; and so much more still, if the calamity was still vastly greater. And why, then, should it be thought unreasonable, and looked upon with a very suspicious eye, as if it must come from some bad cause, when persons are extremely concerned at seeing others in very great danger of suffering the fierceness and wrath of Almighty God to all eternity? And besides, it will doubtless be allowed that those that have very great degrees of the Spirit of God, that is, a spirit of love, may well be supposed to have vastly more of love and compassion to their fellow creatures, than those that are influenced only by common humanity. Why should it be thought strange that those that are full of the Spirit of Christ should be proportionably, in their love to souls, like to Christ? who had so strong a love to them and concern for them as to be willing to drink the dregs of the cup of God's fury for them; and at the same time that he offered up his blood for souls, offered up also, as their high priest, strong crying and tears, with an extreme agony, when the soul of Christ was, as it were, in travail for the souls of the elect; and, therefore, in saving them, he is said to see of the travail of his soul. As such a spirit of love to and concern for souls was the spirit of Christ, so it is the spirit of the church; and, therefore, the church, in desiring and seeking that Christ might be brought forth in the world and in the souls of men, is represented, Rev. xii., as 'a woman crying, travailing in birth, and pained to be delivered.' The spirit of those that have been in distress for the souls of others, so far as I can discern, seems not to be different from that of the apostle, who travailed for souls, and was ready to wish himself accursed from Christ for others. And that of the Psalmist, Psalm cxix. 53, 'Horror hath taken hold upon me, because of the wicked that forsake the law.' And v. 136, 'Rivers of waters run down mine eyes, because they keep not thy law.' And that of the prophet Jeremiah, Jer. iv. 19, 'My bowels! my bowels! I am pained at my very heart; My heart maketh a noise in me: I cannot hold my peace, because thou hast heard. O my soul, the sound of the trumpet, the alarm of war!' And so, chap. ix. 1, and xiii. 17, and Isa. xxii. 4. We read of Mordecai, when he saw his people in danger of being destroyed with a temporal destruction, Esther iv. 1, that he 'rent his clothes, and put on sackcloth and ashes, and went out into the midst of the city, and cried with a loud and bitter cry.['] And why, then, should persons be thought to be distracted, when they cannot forbear crying out at the consideration of the misery of those that are going to eternal destruction?" (Edwards' Works. vol. iv. p. 85. New York edition)

I have read this to show that this thing was common in the great revivals of those days. It has always been so in all great revivals, and has been more or less common in proportion to the greatness, and extent, and depth of the work. It was so in the great revivals in Scotland, and multitudes used to be overpowered, and some almost died, by the depth of their agony.

9. If you mean to pray effectually, you must pray a great deal. It was said of the apostle James, that after he was dead it was found his knees were callous like a camel's knees, by praying so much. Ah! here was the secret of the success of those primitive ministers. They had callous knees.

10. If you intend prayer to be effectual, it must be offered in the name of Christ. You cannot come to God in your own name. You cannot plead your own merits. But you can come in a name that is always acceptable. You all know what it is to use the name of a man. If you should go to the bank with a draft or note, endorsed by John Jacob Astor, that would be giving you his name, and you know you could get the money from the bank just as well as he could himself. Now, Jesus Christ gives you the use of his name. And when

you pray in the name of Christ, the meaning of it is, that you can prevail just as well as he could himself, and receive just as much as God's well-beloved Son would if he were to pray himself for the same things. But you must pray in faith. His name has all the virtue in your lips that it has in his own, and God is just as free to bestow blessings upon you, when you ask in the name of Christ, and in faith, as he would be to bestow them upon Christ, if he should ask.

11. You cannot prevail in prayer, without renouncing all your sins. You must not only recall them to mind, but you must actually renounce them, and leave them off, and in the purpose of your heart renounce them all for ever.

12. You must pray in faith. You must expect to obtain the things you ask for. You need not look for an answer to prayer, if you pray without an expectation of obtaining it. You are not to form such expectations without any reason for them. In the cases I have supposed, there is a reason for the expectation. In case the thing is revealed in God's word, if you pray without an expectation of receiving the blessings, you just make God a liar. If the will of God is indicated by his providence, you ought to depend on it, according to the clearness of the indication, so far as to expect the blessing if you pray for it. And if you are led by his Spirit to pray for certain things, you have just as much reason to expect the thing to be done as if God had revealed it in his word.

But some say, "Will not this view of the leadings of the Spirit of God lead people into fanaticism?" I answer, that I know not but many may deceive themselves in respect to this matter. Multitudes have deceived themselves in regard to all the other points of religion. And if some people should think they are led by the Spirit of God, when it is nothing but their own imagination, is that any reason why those who know that they are led by the Spirit should not follow? Many people suppose themselves to be converted when they are not. Is that any reason why we should not cleave to the Lord Jesus Christ? Suppose some people are deceived in thinking they love God, is that any reason why the pious saint who knows he has the love of God shed abroad in his heart, should not give vent to his feelings in songs of praise? So I suppose some may deceive themselves in thinking they are led by the Spirit of God. But there is no need of being deceived. If people follow impulses, it is their own fault. I do not want you to follow impulses. I want you to be sober minded, and follow the sober, rational leadings of the Spirit of God. There are those who understand what I mean, and who know very well what it is to give themselves up to the Spirit of God in prayer.

III. I will state some of the reasons why these things are essential to effectual prayer. Why does God require such prayer, such strong desires, such agonizing supplications?

1. These strong desires strongly illustrate the strength of God's feelings. They are like the real feelings of God for impenitent sinners. When I have seen, as I sometimes have, the amazing strength of love for souls that has been felt by Christians, I have been wonderfully impressed with the amazing love of God, and his desires for their salvation. The case of a certain woman, of whom I read, in a revival, made the greatest impression on my mind. She had such an unutterable compassion and love for souls, that she actually panted for breath almost to suffocation. What must be the strength of the desire which God feels, when his Spirit produces in Christians such amazing agony, such throes of soul, such travail--God has chosen the best word to express it--it is travail--travail of the soul.

I have seen a man of as much strength of intellect and muscle as any man in the community, fall down prostrate, absolutely overpowered by his unutterable desires for sinners. I know this is a stumbling block to many; and it always will be as long as there remain in the church so many blind and stupid professors of religion. But I cannot doubt that these things are the work of the Spirit of God. Oh that the whole church could be so filled with the Spirit as to travail in prayer, till a nation should be born in a day!

It is said in the word of God, that as soon "as Zion travailed, she brought forth." What does that mean? I asked a professor of religion this question once. He was making exceptions about our ideas of effectual prayer, and I asked him what he supposed was meant by Zion's travailing. "Oh," said he, "it means that as soon as the church walk together in the fellowship of the Gospel, then it will be said that Zion travels! This walking together is called travelling." Not the same term, you see. So much he knew.

2. These strong desires that I have described, are the natural results of great benevolence and clear views of the danger of sinners. It is perfectly reasonable that it should be so. If the women who are in this house should look up there, and see a family burning to death in the fire, and hear their shrieks, and behold their agony, they would feel distressed, and it is very likely that many of them would faint away with agony. And nobody would wonder at it, or say they were fools or crazy to feel so much distressed at such an awful sight. They would think it strange if there were not some expressions of powerful feeling. Why is it any wonder, then, if Christians should feel as I have described, when they have clear views of the state of sinners, and the awful danger they are in? The fact is, that those individuals who never have felt

so, have never felt much real benevolence, and their piety must be of a very superficial character. I do not mean to judge harshly, or to speak unkindly. But I state it as a simple matter of fact; and people may talk about it as they please, but I know that such piety is superficial. This is not censoriousness, but plain truth.

People sometimes wonder at Christians having such feelings. Wonder at what? Why, at the natural, and philosophical, and necessary results of deep piety towards God, and deep benevolence towards man, in view of the great danger they see sinners to be in.

3. The soul of a Christian, when it is thus burdened, must have relief. God rolls this weight upon the soul of a Christian, for the purpose of bringing him near to himself. Christians are often so unbelieving, that they will not exercise proper faith in God, till he rolls this burden upon them, so heavy that they cannot live under it, and then they must go to God for relief. It is like the case of many a convicted sinner. God is willing to receive him at once, if he will come right to him, with faith in Jesus Christ. But the sinner will not come. He hangs back, and struggles, and groans under the burden of his sins, and will not throw himself upon God, till his burden of conviction becomes so great that he can live no longer; and when he is driven to desperation, as it were, and feels as if he was ready to sink into hell, he makes a mighty plunge, and throws himself upon God's mercy as his only hope. It was his duty to come before. God had no delight in his distress, for its own sake. It was only the sinner's obstinacy that created the necessity for all this distress. He would not come without it. So when professors of religion get loaded down with the weight of souls, they often pray again and again, and yet the burden is not gone, nor their distress abated, because they have never thrown it all upon God in faith. But they cannot get rid of the burden. So long as their benevolence continues it will remain and increase, and unless they resist and quench the Holy Ghost they can get no relief, until at length, when they are driven to extremity, they make a desperate effort, roll the burden off upon the Lord Jesus Christ, and exercise a child-like confidence in him. Then they feel relieved; then they feel as if the soul they were praying for would be saved. The burden is gone, and God seems in kindness to sooth down the mind to feel a sweet assurance that the blessing will be granted. Often, after a Christian has had this struggle, this agony in prayer, and has obtained relief in this way, you will find the sweetest and most heavenly affections flow out--the soul rests sweetly and gloriously in God, and rejoices, "with joy unspeakable and full of glory."

Do any of you think now, that there are no such things in the experience of believers? I tell you, if I had time, I could show you from President

Edwards, and other approved writers, cases and descriptions just like this. Do you ask why we never have such things here in New York? I tell you, it is not at all because you are so much wiser than Christians are in the country, or because you have so much more intelligence or more enlarged views of the nature of religion, or a more stable and well regulated piety. I tell you, no; instead of priding yourselves in being free from such extravagances, you ought to hide your heads, because Christians in New York are so worldly, and have so much starch, and pride, and fashion, that they cannot come down to such spirituality as this. I wish it could be so. Oh that there might be such a spirit in this city, and in this church! I know it would make a noise, if we had such things done here. But I would not care for that. Let them say, if they please, that the folks in Chatham Chapel are getting deranged. We need not be afraid of that, if we could live near enough to God to enjoy his Spirit in the manner I have described.

4. These effects of the Spirit of prayer upon the body are themselves no part of religion. It is only that the body is often so weak that the feelings of the soul overpower it. These bodily effects are not at all essential to prevailing prayer, but only a natural or physical result of highly excited emotions of the mind. It is not at all unusual for the body to be weakened and even overcome by any powerful emotion of the mind, on other subjects besides religion. The door-keeper of Congress in the time of the revolution, fell down dead on the reception of some highly cheering intelligence. I knew a woman in Rochester, who was in a great agony of prayer for the conversion of her son-in-law. One morning he was at an anxious meeting, and she remained at home praying for him. At the close of the meeting, he came home a convert, and she was so rejoiced that she fell down and died on the spot. It is no more strange that these effects should be produced by religion than by strong feeling on any other subject. It is not essential to prayer, but the natural result of great effort of the mind.

5. Doubtless one great reason why God requires the exercise of this agonizing prayer is, that it forms such a bond of union between Christ and the Church. It creates such a sympathy between them. It is as if Christ came and poured the overflowings of his own benevolent heart into his church, and led them to sympathize and to co-operate with him, as they never do in any other way. They feel just as Christ feels--so full of compassion for sinners that they cannot contain themselves. Thus it is often with those ministers who are distinguished for their success in preaching to sinners; they often have such compassion, such overflowing desires for their salvation, that it shows itself in their speaking, and their preaching, just as though Jesus Christ spoke through them. The words come from their lips fresh and warm,

as if from the very heart of Christ. I do not mean that he dictates their words; but he excites the feelings that give utterance to them. Then you see a movement in the hearers, as if Christ himself spoke through lips of clay.

6. This travailing in birth for souls creates also a remarkable bond of union between warm-hearted Christians and the young converts. Those who are converted appear very dear to the hearts that have had this spirit of prayer for them. The feeling is like that of a mother for her first-born. Paul expresses it beautifully, when he says, "My little children!" His heart was warm and tender to them. "My little children, of whom I travail in birth again." They had backslidden, and he has all the agonies of a parent over a wandering child. "I travail in birth again, till Christ be formed in you, the hope of glory." In a revival, I have often noticed how those who have had the spirit of prayer, love the young converts. I know this is all algebra to those who have never felt it. But to those who have experienced the agony of wrestling, prevailing prayer, for the conversion of a soul, you may depend upon it, that soul, after it is converted, appears as dear as a child is to the mother who has brought it forth with pain. He has agonized for it, and received it in answer to prayer, and can present it before the Lord Jesus Christ, saying, "Here, Lord, am I, and the children thou hast given me."

7. Another reason why God requires this sort of prayer is, that it is the only way in which the church can be properly prepared to receive great blessings without being injured by them. When the church is thus prostrated in the dust before God, and is in the depth of agony in prayer, the blessing does them good. While at the same time, if they had received the blessing without this deep prostration of soul, it would have puffed them up with pride. But as it is, it increases their holiness, their love, their humility.

IV. I am to show that such prayer as I have described will avail much. But time fails me to go into a particular detail of the evidence which I intended to bring forward under this head.

Elijah the prophet mourned over the declensions of the house of Israel, and when he saw that no other means were likely to be effectual, to prevent a perpetual going away into idolatry, he prayed that the judgments of God might come upon the guilty nation. He prayed that it might not rain, and God shut up the heavens for three years and six months, till the people were driven to the last extremity. And when he saw that it was time to relent, what does he do? See him go up to the mountain and bow down in prayer. He wished to be alone; and he told his servant to go seven times, while he was agonizing in prayer. The last time, the servant told him there was a little cloud appeared, like a man's hand, and he instantly arose from his knees-- the blessing was obtained. The time had come for the calamity to be turned back. "Ah, but," you say, "Elijah was a prophet." Now do not make this objection. They made it in the apostle's days, and what does the apostle say? Why he brought forward this very instance, and the fact that Elijah was a man of like passions with ourselves, as a case of prevailing prayer, and insisted that they should pray so too.

John Knox was a man famous for his power in prayer, so that bloody Queen Mary used to say she feared his prayers more than all the armies of Europe. And events showed that she had reason to do it. He used to be in such an agony for the deliverance of his country that he could not sleep. He had a place in his garden where he used to go to pray. One night he and several friends were praying together, and as they prayed, Knox spoke and said that deliverance had come. He could not tell what had happened, but he felt that something had taken place, for God had heard their prayers. What was it? Why the next news they had was, that Mary was dead!

Take a fact which was related, in my hearing, by a minister. He said, that in a certain town there had been no revival for many years; the church was nearly run out, the youth were all unconverted, and desolation reigned unbroken. There lived in a retired part of the town, an aged man, a blacksmith by trade, and of so stammering a tongue, that it was painful to hear him speak. On one Friday, as he was at work in his shop, alone, his mind became greatly exercised about the state of the church, and of the impenitent. His agony became so great, that he was induced to lay by his work, lock the shop door, and spend the afternoon in prayer.

He prevailed, and on the Sabbath called on the minister, and desired him to appoint a conference meeting. After some hesitation, the minister consented, observing, however, that he feared but few would attend. He appointed it the same evening, at a large private house. When evening came, more assembled than could be accommodated in the house. All was silent for a time, until one sinner broke out in tears, and said, if any one could pray, he begged him to pray for him. Another followed, and another, and still another, until it was found that persons from every quarter of the town were under deep conviction. And what was remarkable was, that they all dated their conviction at the hour when the old man was praying in his shop. A powerful revival followed. Thus this old stammering man prevailed, and, as a prince, had power with God. I could name multitudes of similar cases, but, for want of time, must conclude with a few.

REMARKS.

1. A great deal of prayer is lost, and many people never prevail in prayer, because, when they have desires for particular blessings, they do not follow

them up. They may have had desires, benevolent and pure, which were excited by the Spirit of God; and when they have them, they should persevere in prayer, for if they turn off their attention to other objects, they will quench the Spirit. We tell sinners not to turn off their minds from the one object, but to keep their attention fixed there, till they are saved. When you find these holy desires in your minds, take care of two things:

(1.) Do not quench the Spirit.

(2.) Do not be diverted to other objects.

Follow the leadings of the Spirit, till you have offered that effectual fervent prayer that availeth much.

2. Without the spirit of prayer, ministers will do but little good. A minister need not expect much success, unless he prays for it. Sometimes others may have the spirit of prayer, and obtain a blessing on his labors. Generally, however, those preachers are the most successful who have the most of a spirit of prayer themselves.

3. Not only must ministers have the spirit of prayer, but it is necessary that the church should unite in offering that effectual fervent prayer which can prevail with God. You need not expect a blessing, unless you ask for it. "For all these things will I be inquired of by the house of Israel, to do it."

Now, my brethren, I have only to ask you, in regard to what I have preached to-night, "Will you do it?" Have you done what I preached to you last Friday evening? Have you gone over with your sins, and confessed them, and got them all out of the way? Can you pray now? And will you join and offer prevailing prayer, that the Spirit of God may come down here?

Chapter Three

Pilgrims' Prayers

After years of persecution for their faith in 1620, 102 Separatists embarked upon a dangerous, ocean voyage. Their ship, the Mayflower, sailed through some of the worst winter storms of that era. There were 13 women on board, and three of them were pregnant. There was no privacy, no sanitation and a plague was working its way through the crew. Before they embarked, they prayed and asked God for safe passage and promised that if they reached their destination they would establish a base for world evangelism of the Gospel of Jesus Christ. Several times during the crossing, they thought they were going to sink, but their prayers before, during and after the voyage were answered, and they reached Plymouth.

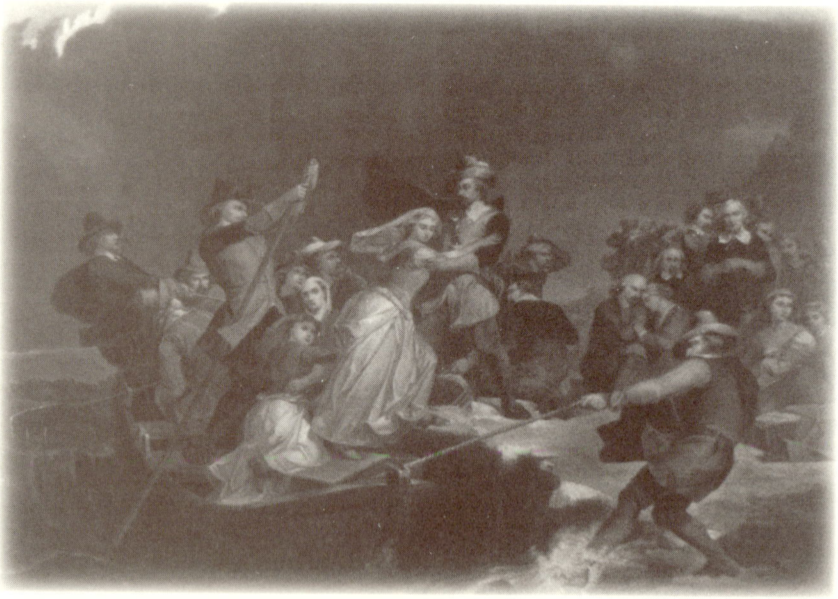

William Bradford's
Of Plimoth (Plymouth) Plantation 1620-1647
(from original manuscript)

Those living in England in 1608 who were considered dissenters were often refused the mandatory license when seeking to go abroad.

Being thus constrained to leave their native soyle and countrie, their lands & livings, and all their freinds and famillier acquaintance, it was much; and thought marvelous by many. But to goe into a countrie they knew not (but by hearsay), wher they must learne a new language, and get their livings they knew not how…was by many thought an adventure almost desperate, a case intolerable, & a miserie worse than death…But these things did not dismay them…for their desires were sett on ye ways of God, & to injoye his ordinances; but they rested on his providence, & knew whom they had beleeved. Yet this was not all, for though they could not stay, yet were ye not suffered to goe, but ye ports & havens were shut against them, so as they were faine to seeke secrete means of conveance, & to bribe & fee the mariners, & give exterordinairie rates for their passages. And yet were they often times betrayed…they & their goods intercepted & surprised, and thereby put to great trouble and charge…
(Chapter II)

Finally arriving in Holland, the Pilgrims settled here for almost twelve years of religious freedom. Seeking a better country for their children, their eyes turned to the New World.

AND first after their humble praiers unto God for his direction & assistance, & a generall conference held here aboute, they consulted what perticuler place to pitch upon, & prepare for. Some…had thoughts & were ernest for Guiana, or some of those fertill places in those hott climats; others were for some parts of Virginia, wher ye English had already made enterance, & beginning…if they lived among ye English wch wear ther planted, or so near them as to be under their government, they should be in as great danger to be troubled and persecuted for the cause of religion, as if they lived in England,

THE MAYFLOWER AT SEA.

and it might be worse...But at length ye conclusion was, to live as a distincte body by them selves, under ye generall Government of Virginia; and by their freinds to sue to his majestie that he would be pleased to grant them freedome of Religion...
(Chapter V)

...Ye kings majestie was willing enough to suffer them without molestation, though for other reasons he would not confirme it by any publick acte.
(Chapter V)

UPON ye receite of these things by one of their messengers, they had a sollemne meeting and a day of humilliation to seek ye Lord for his direction...
(Chapter VI)

1620
So being ready to departe, they had a day of solleme humiliation, their pastor taking his texte from Ezra...The rest of the time was spente in powering out prairs to ye Lord with great fervencie, mixed with abundance of tears... So they lefte yt goodly & pleasante citie, which had been ther resting place near 12. years; but they knew they were pilgrimes, & looked not much on those things, but lift up their eyes to ye heavens, their dearest cuntrie, and quieted their spirits.
(Chapter VII)

September 1620
...And now all being compacte togeather in one shipe, they put to sea againe with a prosperus winde, which continued diverce days togeather, which was some incouragemente unto them...After they had injoyed faire winds and weather for a season, they were incountered many times with crosse winds, and mette with many feirce stormes...So they comited them selves to ye will of God, & resolved to proseede. In sundrie of these stormes the winds were so feirce, & ye seas so high, as they could not beare a knote of saile, but were forced to hull (drift with the wind under very short sail) for diverce days togither...In all this viage ther died but one of ye passengers...
(Chapter IX)

November 11, 1620 (65 days since departing)
And ye next day they gott into ye Cape-harbor wher they ridd in safetie... Being thus arived in a good harbor and brought safe to land, they fell upon their knees & blessed ye God of heaven, who had brought them over ye vast

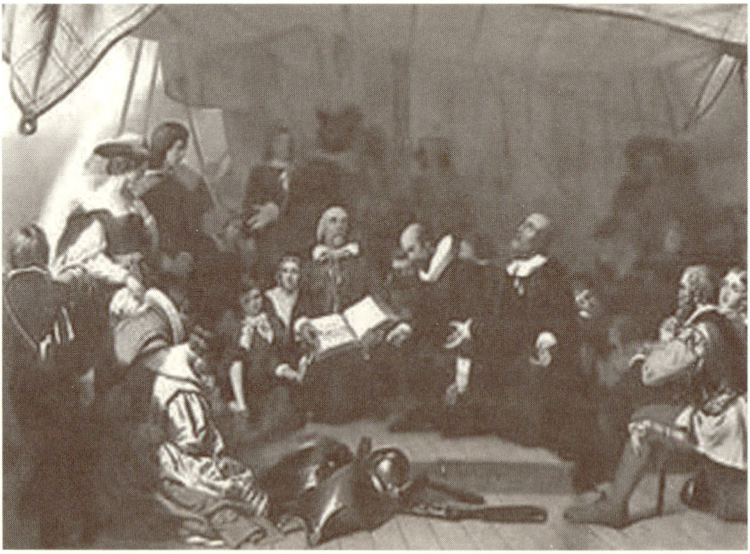

& furious ocean, and delivered them from all ye periles & miseries thereof... But hear I cannot but stay and make a pause, and stand half amased at this poore peoples presente condition; and so I thinke will the reader too, when he well considers ye same. Being thus passed ye vast ocean, and a sea of troubles before in their preparation...they had now no freinds to wellcome them, nor inns to entertaine or refresh their weatherbeaten bodys, no houses or much less townes to repair too, to seeke for succoure...What could now sustaine them but ye spirite of God & his grace?

December 6, 1620 Third Scouting Expedition

The month of November being spente in these affairs, & much foule weather falling in, the 6. of Desem: they sente out their shallop againe with 10. of their principall men, & some sea men, upon further discovery, intending to circulate that deepe bay of Cape-codd. The weather was very could, & it frose so hard as ye sprea of ye sea lighting on their coats, they were as if they had been glased; yet that night betimes they gott downe into ye botome of ye bay, and as they drue nere ye shore they saw some 10. or 12. Indeans very busie aboute some thing. They landed aboute a league or 2. from them, and had much a doe to put a shore any wher, it lay so full of flats. Being landed, it grew late, and they made them selves a barricade with loggs & bowes...When morning was come...they ranged up and doune all yt day...When ye sune grue low, they hasted out of ye woods...made them a barricado...So they rested till about 5. of ye clock in the morning...after praier they prepared for breakfast, and it being day dawning, it was thought best to be carring things downe to ye boate...But presently, all on ye sudain, they heard a great & strange crie, which they knew to be the same voyces they heard in ye night, though they varied their notes, & one of their company being abroad came runing in, & cried, "Men, Indeans, Indeans"; and wthal, their arowes came flying amongst them. Their men rane with all speed to recover their armes, as by ye good providence of God they did...Thus it pleased God to vanquish their enimies and give them deliverance; and by His spetiall providence so to dispose that not any one of them were either hurte, or hitt, though their arrows came close by them, & on every side them; and sundry of their coats, which hung up in ye barricado, were shot throw & throw. Afterwards they gave God sollamne thanks and praise for their deliverance, & gathered up a bundle of their arrows, & sent them into England afterward by ye mr. of ye ship, and called that place ye first encounter. From hence they departed, & costed all along, but discerned no place likly for harbor...After some houres sailing, it begane to snow & raine, & about ye middle of ye afternoone, ye wind increased, & ye sea became very rough, and they broake their rudder, & it was as much as 2. men could doe to steere her with a cupple of oares...they broake their mast in

SAMOSET WELCOMING THE ENGLISH.

3. peeces, & their saill fell over bord, in a very grown sea, so as they had like to have been cast away; yet by Gods mercie they recovered them selves…And though it was very darke, and rained sore, yet in ye end they gott under ye lee of a small island…

(Chapter X)

But that which was most sadd & lamentable was, that in 2. or 3. moneths time halfe of their company dyed, espetialy in Jan: & February, being ye depth of winter, and wanting houses & other comforts; being infected with ye scurvie & other diseases, which this long vioage & their inacomodate condition had brought upon them…ther was but 6. or 7. sound persons, who, to their great comendations be it spoken, spared no pains, night nor day, but with abundance of toyle and hazard of their owne health, fetched them woode, made them fires, drest them meat, made their beads, washed their lothsome cloaths…shewing herein their true love unto their freinds & brethren…the Lord so upheld these persons, as in this generall calamity they were not at all infected either with sickness, or lamnes. And what I have said of these, I may say of many others who dyed in this general vissitation, & others yet living, that whilst they had health, yea, or any strength continuing, they were not wanting to any that had need of them. And I doute not but their recompence is with ye Lord.

But about ye 16. of March, a certaine Indian came boldly amongst them, and spoke to them in broken English…he told them also of another Indian whos name was Squanto, a native of this place, who had been in England & could speake better English then him selfe…a while after he came againe… with the aforesaid Squanto…Squanto contiued with them, and was their interpreter, and was a spetiall instrument sent of God for their good beyond their expectation. He directed them how to set their corne, wher to take fish, and to procure other comodities, and was also their pilott to bring them to unknowne places for their profitt, and never left them till he dyed.

September 1621

And thus they found ye Lord to be with them in all their ways, and to blesse their outgoings & incomings, for which let his holy name have ye praise for ever, to all posteritie. They begane now to gather in ye small harvest they had, and to fitte up their houses and dwellings against winter, being all well recovered in health & strengt, and had all things in good plenty…All ye somer ther was no wante. And now begane to come in store of foule, as winter

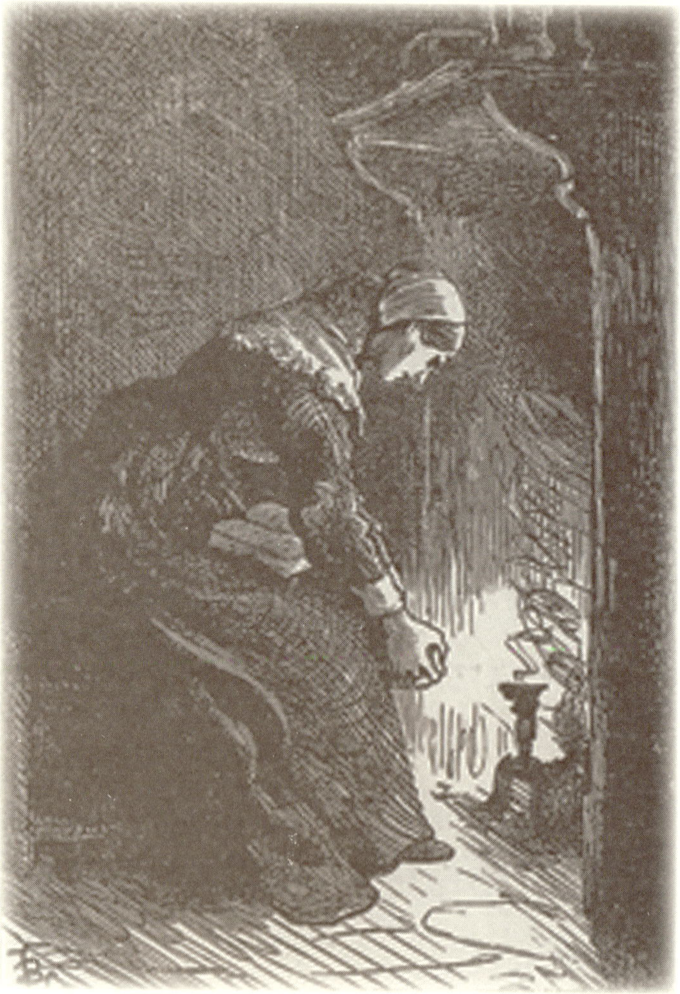

aproached, of which this place did abound when they came first...And besids water foule, ther was great store of wild Turkies, of which they tooke many, besides venison, &c. Besids they had aboute a peck a meale a weeke to a person, or now since harvest, Indean corne to yt proportion.

1622

Althings being provided...Squanto fell sick of an Indean feavor...and within a few days dyed ther; desiring ye Gov to pray for him, that he might goe to ye Englishmens God in Heaven; and bequeathed sundrie of his things to sundry of his English friends, as remembrances of his love; of whom they had a great loss.

May 1623

...the Lord seemed to blast...from ye 3. weeke in May, till about ye midle of July, without any raine, and with great heat (for ye most parte), insomuch as ye corne begane to wither away, though it was set with fishe...Yet at length it begane to languish sore, and some of ye drier grounds were partched like withered hay...Upon which they sett a parte a solemne day of humilliation, to seek the Lord by humble & fervente prayer, in this great distrese. And he was pleased to give them a gracious & speedy answer, both to their owne, and the Indeans admiration, that lived amongest them. For all ye morning, and greatest part of the day, it was clear weather & very hotte, and not a cloud or any signe of raine to be seen, yet toward evening it begane to overcast, and shortly after to raine with shuch sweete and gentle showers, as gave them cause of rejoyceing, & blessing God. It came, without either wind, or thunder, or any violence, and by degreese in yt abundance, as that ye earth was thorowly wete and soked...Which did so apparently revive & quicken ye decayed corne & other fruits, as was wonderfull to see, and made the Indeans astonished to behold: and afterwards the Lord sent them shuch seasonable showers, with enterchange of faire warme weather, as, through his blessing, caused a fruitfull and liberall harvest, to their no small comforte and rejoycing.

Chapter Four

Political Prayers

Chaplain Prayers of the House and Senate

The opening prayer of each Congressional session of the House and the Senate has its beginnings in the days of the Continental Congress June 28, 1787.

The delegates at the Constitutional Convention were trying to compose the United States Constitution in an attempt to give us "a more perfect union". After five weeks of heated discussion nothing had been accomplished. Our fledgling Nation had thirteen states which had different monetary systems, different tariffs, and different foreign policies. Approximately half of the people lived in three states and the other half lived in ten states. The leadership in some states wanted slavery and some did not; there was an impasse. The meeting started to break up and George Mason, an influential delegate, got up and started to walk out. George Washington, the President of the Convention, walked out with him. Washington convinced Mason to come back because Dr. Franklin was about to address the Convention. He was one of six out of the fifty-six who had made it back from the signing of the Declaration to the same room to draft the Constitution. Sick and in his eighties, he rose to speak and to give the following address:

BENJAMIN FRANKLIN.

"In this situation of this Assembly, groping as it were in the dark to find political truth, and scarce able to distinguish it when presented to us, how has it happened, sir, that we have not hitherto once thought of humbly applying to the Father of Lights to illuminate our understanding? In the beginning of the contest with Great Britain, when we were sensible of danger, we had daily prayer in this room for the Divine protection. Our prayers, sir, were heard, and they were graciously answered. All of us who were engaged in the struggle must have observed frequent instances of a superintending Providence in our favor. . . And have we now forgotten that powerful Friend? Or do we imagine we no longer need His assistance? I have lived, sir, a long time, and the longer I live, the more convincing proofs I see of this truth – that God governs in the affairs of men. And if a sparrow cannot fall to the ground without His notice, is it probable that an empire can rise without His aid? We have been assured, sir, in the Sacred Writings, that "except the Lord build the House, they labor in vain that build it." I firmly believe this; and I also believe that without His concurring aid we shall succeed in this political building no better than the builders of Babel. . .I therefore beg leave to move that henceforth prayers imploring the assistance of Heaven, and its blessings on our deliberations, be held in this Assembly every morning before we proceed to business, and that one or more of the Clergy of this City be requested to officiate in that Service."

What Ben Franklin was telling the Convention delegates with all their intelligence, purpose, and sacrifice was that they had forgotten the most important thing; prayer! With that address finished, the Constitutional Convention adjourned and for the next three days many of the delegates walked across the street, prayed, fasted, and attended church services. When they reconvened, there was a completely different tenor among the delegates. Several weeks later, the most remarkable governmental document in the history of mankind was completed.

The Prayer in the First Congress, 1774

The first time the Continental Congress met, they realized our young Country was going to be facing some grave challenges. For this reason they prayed for hours while reading Psalm 35. The beginning prayer was given by Jacob Duché.

O Lord our Heavenly Father, high and mighty King of kings, and Lord of lords, who dost from thy throne behold all the dwellers on earth and reignest with power supreme and uncontrolled over all the Kingdoms, Empires and Governments; look down in mercy, we beseech Thee, on these our American States, who have fled to Thee from the rod of the oppressor and thrown themselves on Thy gracious protection, desiring to be henceforth dependent only on Thee. To Thee have they appealed for the righteousness of their cause; to Thee do they now look up for that countenance and support, which Thou alone canst give. Take them, therefore, Heavenly Father, under Thy nurturing care; give them wisdom in Council and valor in the field; defeat the malicious designs of our cruel adversaries; convince them of the unrighteousness of their Cause and if they persist in their sanguinary purposes, of own unerring justice, sounding in their hearts, constrain them to drop the weapons of war from their unnerved hands in the day of battle!

Be Thou present, O God of wisdom, and direct the councils of this honorable assembly; enable them to settle things on the best and surest foundation. That the scene of blood may be speedily closed; that order, harmony and peace may be effectually restored, and truth and justice, religion and piety, prevail and flourish amongst the people. Preserve the health of their bodies and vigor of their minds; shower down on them and the millions they here represent, such temporal blessings as Thou seest expedient for them in this world and crown them with everlasting glory in the world to come. All this we ask in the name and through the merits of Jesus Christ, Thy Son and our Savior. Amen.

The Rev. Jacob Duché led the first prayer for the Second Continental Congress, Philadelphia, September 7, 1774.

John Adams' Letter to His Wife after the First Session of Congress
16 September 1774

Having a Leisure Moment, while the Congress is assembling, I gladly embrace it to write you a Line.

When the Congress first met, Mr. Cushing made a Motion, that it should be opened with Prayer. It was opposed by Mr. Jay of N. York and Mr. Rutledge of South Carolina, because we were so divided in religious Sentiments, some Episcopalians, some Quakers, some Aanabaptists, some Presbyterians and some Congregationalists, so that We could not join in the same Act of Worship.-Mr. S. Adams arose and said he was no Bigot, and could hear a Prayer from a Gentleman of Piety and Virtue, who was at the same Time a Friend to his Country. He was a Stranger in Phyladelphia, but had heard that Mr. Duche deserved that Character, and therefore he moved that Mr. Duche, an episcopal Clergyman, might be desired, to read Prayers to the Congress, tomorrow Morning. The Motion was seconded and passed in the Affirmative. Mr. Randolph our President, waited on Mr. Duche, and received for Answer that if his Health would permit, he certainly would. Accordingly next Morning he appeared with his Clerk and in his Pontificallibus, and read several Prayers, in the established Form; and then read the Collect for the seventh day of September, which was the Thirty fifth Psalm. -You must remember this was the next Morning after we heard the horrible Rumour, of the Cannonade of Boston.-I never saw a greater Effect upon an Audience. It seemed as if Heaven had ordained that Psalm to be read on that Morning. After this Mr. Duche, unexpected to every Body struck out into an extemporary Prayer, which filled the Bosom of every Man present. I must confess I never heard a better Prayer or one, so well pronounced. Episcopalian as he is, Dr. Cooper himself never prayed with such fervour, such Ardor, such Earnestness and Pathos, and in Language so elegant and sublime-for America, for the Congress, for The Province of Massachusetts Bay, and especially the Town of Boston. It has had an excellent Effect upon every Body here. I must beg you to read that Psalm. If there was any Faith in

the sortes Virgilianae, or sortes Homericae, or especially the Sortes biblicae, it would be thought providential. It will amuse your Friends to read this Letter and the 35th. Psalm to them. Read it to your Father and Mr. Wibirt.-I wonder what our Braintree Churchmen would think of this?-Mr. Duche is one of the most ingenious Men, and best Characters, and greatest orators in the Episcopal order, upon this Continent-Yet a Zealous Friend of Liberty and his Country. I long to see my dear Family. God bless, preserve and prosper it.
Adieu.
John Adams

From that advent of that first prayer Congress has never met, even if it has been for a few minutes without going to the Lord in prayer…

The Prayers of Rev. Peter Marshall before the U.S. Senate

Reverend Peter Marshall was appointed the Chaplain of the United States Senate in the 1940s. He was an immigrant from Scotland and loved his adopted homeland. As he stood before the Senate, Peter Marshall had an excellent way of expressing what American exceptionalism is by describing the virtues of honesty, integrity, and liberty in his prayers. When Peter Marshall was there to open the Senate in prayer, the Senators would make a special effort to be present to hear him articulate another sacred message to God.

Prayers for the Nation

Lord Jesus, thou who art the way, the truth, and the life; hear us as we pray for the truth that shall make all free. Teach us that liberty is not only to be loved but also to be lived. Liberty is too precious a thing to be buried in books. It costs too much to be hoarded. Help us see that our liberty is not the right to do as we please, but the opportunity to please to do what is right.

America Confesses

Our Father, bring to the remembrance of Thy people Thine ancient time-honored promise: "If my people, which are called by my name, shall humble themselves, and pray, and seek my face, and turn from their wicked ways; then will I hear from heaven, and will forgive their sin, and will heal their land." We, this company of Thy people assembled, would begin now to meet the conditions that will enable Thee to fulfill Thy promise. May all of America come to understand that right-living alone exalteth a nation, that only in Thy will can peace and joy be found. But, Lord, this land cannot be righteous unless her people are righteous, and we, here gathered, are part of America. We know that the world cannot be changed until the hearts of man are changed. Our hearts need to be changed. We therefore confess to Thee that: Wrong ideals and sinful living have cut us off from Thee. We have been greedy. We have sought to hide behind barricades of selfishness; shackles have imprisoned the great heart of America. We have tried to isolate ourselves from the bleeding wounds of a blundering world. In our self-sufficiency we have sought not Thy help. We have held conferences and ignored Thee completely. We have disguised selfishness as patriotism; our arrogance has masqueraded as pride. We have fritted away time and opportunities while the world bled. Our ambitions have blinded us to opportunities. We have bickered in factory and business, and sought to solve our differences only through self-interest. Lord God of Hosts, forgive us! O God, by Thy guidance and Thy power may our beloved land once again become God's one country, a nation contrite in heart, confessing her sins, a nation keenly sensitive to all the unresolved injustice and wrong still in our midst. Hear this our prayer and grant that we may confidently expect to see it answered in our time, through Jesus Christ, our Lord. Amen.

For God's Grace in Our Helplessness

We know, our Father, that at this desperate hour in world affairs, we need Thee. We need Thy strength, Thy guidance, Thy wisdom. There are problems far greater than any wisdom of man can solve. What shall our leaders do in such an hour? May Thy wisdom and Thy power come upon the President of these United States, the Senators and Congressmen, to whom have been entrusted leadership. May the responsibility lie heavily on their hearts, until they are ready to acknowledge their helplessness and turn to Thee. Give to them the honest, the courage, and the moral integrity to confess that they don't know what to do. Only then can they lead us as a nation beyond human wisdom to Thee, who alone hast the answer. Lead us to this high adventure. Remind us that a "mighty fortress is our God" – not a hiding place where we can escape for an easy life, but rather an arsenal of courage and strength – the mightiest of all, who will march beside us into the battle for righteousness and world brotherhood. O our God, may we never recover from our feeling of helplessness and our need of Thee! In the strong name of Jesus, our Lord, we pray. Amen.

For the President of the United States

We pray, Lord Jesus, for our President. We are deeply concerned that he may know the will of God, and that he may have the spiritual courage and grace to follow it. Deliver him, we pray, from all selfish considerations. Lift him above the claims of politics. Fill him with the Spirit of God that shall make him fearless to seek, to know, to do the right. Save him from the friends who, in the name of politics or even friendship, would persuade him from that holy path. Strengthen and empower his advisers. Bring them, too, to their knees in prayer. May their example and their influence spread, that we, in these United States, may yet have a government of men who know Thee, the Almighty God, as their Friend, and who place Thy will first in their lives as well as in their prayers. Hear and answer, we pray Thee, forgiving us all our unworthiness; cleansing us from every ignoble thought and unworthy ambition that we may be renewed in spirit and mind and heart, through Jesus Christ, our Lord. Amen.

THE WHITE HOUSE AT WASHINGTON.

For the Leaders of Our Nation

Our Father, bless, we pray Thee, the leaders of this nation. Strengthen the courage of the representatives in Congress assembled – sincere men who want to do the right, if only they can be sure what is right. Make it plain to them, O Lord. And then wilt Thou start them out on the right way, for Thou knowest that we are hard to turn. Forgive them for the blunders they have committed, the compromises they have made. Give to them the courage to admit mistakes. Take away from us as a nation and as individuals that stubborn pride which, followed by conceit, imagines itself to be above and beyond criticism. Save our leaders, O God, from themselves and from their friends – even as Thou hast saved them from their enemies. Let no personal ambition blind them to their opportunities. Help them to give battle to hypocrisy wherever they find it. Give them divine common sense and a selflessness that shall make them think of service and not of gain. May they have the courage to lead the people of this Republic, considering unworthy the expediency of following the people. Save them from the folly of man-made schemes and plans. Give to them the faith and the courage together to seek God's inspired plan and, finding it, to propose it, knowing that when it is God-inspired, Thou wilt open the way for it through all obstacles. As Thou hast made and preserved us a nation, so now mold us into a people more worthy of a great heritage. In Thy strong name we make these prayers. Amen.

Prayer for America

Our Father, we pray for this land. We need Thy help in this time of testing and uncertainty, when men who could fight together on the field of battle seem strangely unable to work together around conference tables for peace. May we begin to see that all true Americanism begins in being Christian; that it can have no other foundation, as it has no other roots. To Thy glory was this Republic established. For the advancement of the Christian faith did the Founding Fathers give their life's heritage, passed down to us.
We would pray that all over this land there may be a return to the faith of those men and women who trusted God as they faced the perils and dangers of the frontier, not alone in crossing the continent, in building their cabins, in rearing their families, in eking out a livelihood, but in raising a standard of faith to which men have been willing to repair down through the years. Thou didst bless their efforts. Thou didst bless America. Thou hast made her rich. Wilt Thou also make her good? Make us, the citizens of this land, what to do the right things. Make us long to have right attitudes. Help us to be Chris-

tian in our attitudes. Let all that we do and say spring out of understanding hearts. Make us willing to seek moral objectives together, that in united action this nation may be as resolute for righteousness and peace as she has been for war. Bless those who bear responsibility. May they be led by Thee to do that which is right rather than that which is expedient or politically wise. Save us from politicians who seek only their own selfish interests. Illumine the minds of management as well as labor, that there may be an end to selfishness and greed, to the stupidity of men who are unable to find in reasonable agreement solutions to the problems that plague us. Bless this land that we love so much, our Father, and help her to deposit her trust, not in armies and navies, in wealth and material resources, or in achievements of the human mind, but in that righteousness which alone exalteth any nation, and by which alone peace can finally come to us. This we ask in that name that is above every name, Thy Son, Jesus Christ, our Redeemer. Amen.

For Those in Service of Our Country

We, LORD, Jesus, are children of God. Yet we would not be the sons and daughters of men were we not sometimes fearful, did not our hearts often ache and harbor anxiety for those we love who wear our country's uniform, who serve her in distant places. Yet we know, our Father, that the Everlasting Arms reach out across the world. We know that the shadow of Thy wing covers all Thy children. We are persuaded that in that world of the Spirit in which we really live neither persecution nor peril nor sword shall be able to separate us from Thy love. We know that the bonds of fellowship of prayer are real. We know that at the throne of grace we are all united, that our souls mingle with those we love on earth even though separated by tumbling sea and dreary miles. So now our minds and hearts reach out to be in spirit with those whom we name now before Thee; to surround them with our love and prayers and hopes. For them we ask:

Support in time of need…Strength beyond their own…Confidence that Thou are their Shepherd, that Thou wilt never for a moment forsake them…Thy strength in temptation, that they may be kept clean…The gift of inner peace, a serenity that no tragedy can destroy…That knowledge of God that shall assure them of eternal life, of peace and joy forevermore…Thy gift of resoluteness in duty; gird them with courage; enable them to quit themselves like men who have deposited all their trust in their God…A determination toward love, not hatred, that the fruits of victory shall not wither…Salvation of body and soul, and if it be possible, bring them safely home. We thank Thee that this ministry of intercessory prayer has linked our hearts and bound us even closer to those we love – closer to Thee and to them. May we feel Thy presence, and see by faith that day when the love of Christ shall live in the hearts of all men everywhere. Hear, O God, not alone these prayers, but the unspoken inarticulate yearning of every seeking heart bowed before Thee. In the name of Jesus Christ, our Lord. Amen.

In a Time of National Danger

O LORD, when we, Thy children, are apprehensive about the affairs of our world, remind us that Thou are in Thy world as well as above and beyond it. Remind us that Thou art not indifferent. For Thou art not a spectator God, high and lifted up, serene an unperturbed. The feet that were wounded are still walking the trails of earth. The heart that was broken on the tree still feels every human woe. Thus shall we not feel forsaken, nor give way to hopelessness. Thus we shall know that Thou hast a plan, and that Thy will shall one day be done on earth, not alone by those who love Thee and know Thee to be God, but by all, not in one nation or two, but in all the nations of the earth. Then shall every tongue confess that Christ is Lord, and every knee shall bow before Thee. Sustain us with that hope and encouragement, that our prayer be not in vain when we pray "Thy Kingdom come." Come it will, however dark may be the present prospects for peace on earth – in the darkness of men's minds and the hardness of men's hearts. We do pray that Thou, O Holy Spirit, where Thou dost find the doors of human hearts still closed before Thee, wilt knock the louder and wilt, in Thy own secret way, prevail upon the wills of men that they may do the will of God – ere it be too late. All these things we ask in that name above every name, that name before whom all nations of the earth shall bow, Thy son, Jesus Christ, our Redeemer. Amen.

Before a National Election

LORD Jesus, we ask Thee to guide the people of this nation as they exercise their dearly bought privilege of franchise. May it neither be ignored unthinkingly nor undertaken lightly. As citizens all over this land go to the ballot boxes, give them a sense of high privilege and joyous responsibility. Help those who are about to be elected to public office to come to understand the real source of their mandate – a mandate given by no party machine, received at no polling booth, but given by God; a mandate to govern wisely and well; a mandate to represent God and truth at the heart of the nation; a mandate to do good in the name of Him under whom this Republic was established. We ask Thee to lead America in the paths where Thou wouldst have her walk, to do the tasks which Thou hast laid before her. So may we together seek happiness for all our citizens in the name of Him who created us all equal in His sight, and therefore brothers. Amen.

For a Renaissance of Faith

Our Father, remove from us the sophistication of our age and the skepticism that has come, like frost, to blight our faith and to make it weak. Bring us back to a faith that makes men great and strong, a faith that enables us to love and to live, the faith by which we are triumphant, the faith by which alone we can walk with Thee. We pray for a return of that simple faith, that old-fashioned faith, that made strong and great the homes of our ancestors who built this good land and who in building left us our heritage. In the strong name of Jesus, our Lord, we make this prayer. Amen.

Rev. Peter Marshall, Chaplain of the U.S. Senate

Tuesday, Feb. 11, 1947

We thank thee, Almighty God, for the rich heritage of this good land; for the evidences of Thy favor in the past; and for the Hand that hath made and preserved us a nation. We thank thee for the men and women who, by blood and sweat, by toil and tears, forged on the anvil of their own sacrifice all that we hold dear. May we never lightly esteem what they obtained at a great price. Grateful for rights and privileges, may we be conscious of duties and obligations.

On this day we thank Thee for the inspiration that breathes in the memory of Abraham Lincoln, and we pray that something of the spirit that was his may be ours today. Like him, may we be more concerned that we are on Thy side, than that Thou art on ours. In our hearts may there be, as there was in his, malice toward none and charity for all; that we may, together, with Thy blessing and help, bind up the Nation's wounds, and do all which may achieve and cherish a just and lasting peace among ourselves and with all nations. Through Jesus Christ our Lord. Amen.

Wednesday, April 9, 1947

Our Fathers' God to Thee, who art the author of our liberty, and under whom we have our freedom, we make our prayer. Make us ever mindful of the price that was paid to obtain that freedom and the cost that must be met to keep it. Help us in this Nation so to live it that other men shall desire it and seek after it. Believing in it, give us the backbone to stand up for it. Loving it, may we be willing to defend it. In the strong name of Him who said, "If ye continue in My word, ye shall know the truth, and the truth shall make you free." Amen.

Friday, April 18, 1947

Our Father, we yearn for a better understanding of spiritual things, that we may know surely what Thy will is for us and for our Nation. Give to us clear vision that we may know where to stand and what to stand for—because unless we stand for something, we shall fall for anything. Remind us, O God, that Thou hast not resigned. Harassed and troubled by the difficulties and uncertainties of the hour, we rest our minds on Thee, who dost not change. May it ever be in our minds as upon our coins that in God we trust. For Jesus' sake. Amen.

Thursday, April 24, 1947

Our Father, we in this place are weighed down by the problems of our nation and of our world. Convict us of our share of personal responsibility for the situation in which we find ourselves. May we confess our part in creating our dilemmas, lest we feel no obligation to solve them. Help us to quit waiting for the other fellow to change his attitude and his ways, lest we never give Thee the chance for which Thou hast been waiting to change us. This we ask in the lovely name of Him who came to change us all, even Jesus Christ our Lord. Amen.

Friday, April 25, 1947

Our Father which art in Heaven, we pray for all the people of our country, that they may learn to appreciate more the goodly heritage that is ours. We need to learn, in these challenging days, that to every right there is attached a duty and to every privilege an obligation. We believe that, in the eternal order of things, Thou hast so ordained it, and what Thou hast joined together let us not try to put asunder. Teach us what freedom is. May we all learn the lesson that it is not the right to do as we please, but the opportunity to please to do what is right. Above, all, may we discover that wherever the Spirit of the Lord is there is freedom. May we have that freedom now, in His presence here, to lead us and to help us keep this Nation free. This we ask in Jesus' name. Amen

The following excerpts of other prayers are taken from dark times within our National history.

1861 (July 4), Senate Prayer

The Chaplin, Rev. Byron Sunderland, D.D., offered the following prayer:

Almighty and everlasting God, be not angry with us for our sins, which we only confess and deplore; but pardon our offenses and extend to us Thy favor. We thank Thee for Thy goodness on this anniversary of the nation a day tenfold more precious by reason of our present troubles, and sacred to the heart for the ever memorable Declaration of our fathers, in which Thou didst begin more openly to give us a name among the nations of the earth. We thank Thee for all Thy manifold and abundant mercies hitherto to make our nation exceedingly great and glorious; but now disasters have befallen us and darkness broods in the land. And now we ask Thy mercy as the Senate is convening at a most momentous crisis of our history. Give to Thy servants all needed help. Add to their deliberations wisdom and unanimity, and profit and speed to their conclusion. Bless Thy servant, the President of the United States, our veteran Commander-in-Chief, and all that have functions in the civil and military power. May the angel of Thy presence walk in the Cabinet and in the Congress and in the camp, to go before, to purify, and to direct the now greatly and universally-awakened love of country. And we beseech Thee to guide us, to overrule and order all things, and so to cause that nothing shall fail, that the disorders of the land may be speedily healed, that peace and concord may prevail, that truth and righteousness may be established, and that Thy Church and Kingdom may flourish in a larger peace and prosperity, for Thy Son, our Saviour, Jesus Christ's sake. Amen. (Source: Congressional Globe, 37th Congress, first session, new series, 1, 4 July 1861.)

1918 (July 4), House Prayer

The Chaplain, Rev. Henry N. Couden, D.D., offered the following prayer:

Our Father in Heaven, the inspiration of every generous impulse, every high and noble aspiration, we thank Thee from our heart of hearts for the "Spirit of '76," which gave to us the immortal Declaration of Independence, which led on to victory and the formation of our Glorious Republic, which has not only been the wonder but the admiration of the world. We thank Thee for the day which will be celebrated with more than usual interest throughout the length and breadth of the land. The native born and the naturalized citizen will vie with each other in making it memorable. For the first time in its history it will be celebrated by our sister nations, who are engaged with us in fighting for the same principles for which our forefathers fought, in a world-wide war for humanity, liberty, justice, and equal rights for all mankind.

May it furnish new inspiration to us and our allies, which will bring victory to their arms; then an everlasting peace; to the glory and honor of Thy Holy Name. Amen. (Source: Congressional Record-House, 65th Congress, second session, 56/9, July 4, 1918, 8668.)

1943 (July 5), Senate Prayer

The Chaplain, Rev. Frederick Brown Harris, D.D., offered the following prayer:

Our fathers' God and ours, on the birthday of national independence we confess our dependence upon Thee. Without Thee we are lost in spite of the overwhelming might of our national arms. We thank Thee for those pilgrims of faith who came hither in their frail barque across mountainous seas and who stepped upon strange shores with the salutation to a new world, "In the Name of God. Amen." The Nation here established, conceived in liberty and dedicated to the proposition that all men are created equal has acknowledged that Name above every name and reverenced it, has built its altars, reared its temples, and raised its steeples, emblems of a faith that points to the skies and wings its sure and certain way to God. Make that faith of the fathers, we pray, real to us in these tempestuous days. Save us from a freedom of speech so empty that we have nothing worth saying, from a freedom of worship so futile that we have no God to adore, from freedom from want and fear with no creative idea as to how to use our plenty or our security for the redemption of our social order and for the salvation of our own souls. Let all that is low and unworthy in us sink to the depths. Let all that is high and fine in us rise to greet the morn of a new day confident that the best is yet to be. Amen. (Source: Congressional Record- Senate, 78th Congress, first session, 89/5, July 5, 1943, 7160.)

1962 (July 5), House Prayer

The Chaplain, Rev. Bernard Braskamp, D.D., offered the following prayer:

Psalm 11: 3: If the foundations be destroyed what can the righteous do?
O Thou Eternal God, may our minds and hearts be stirred with a deepening sense of patriotism and gratitude as we continue to think of that day of high and holy memory in our national history when a company of God-fearing men were guided by Thy divine wisdom to sign the Declaration of Independence. Grant that the blessings of freedom, which were purchased at a tremendous cost and which we prize so highly and are privileged to enjoy in such an abundant measure, may always be coordinated with the spirit of self-discipline.

Help us to cling with increasing tenacity of faith and fortitude to the great truth proclaimed by George Washington in his Farewell Address that religion and morality are indispensable and our national greatness if we allow them to be subverted and obliterated by secularism. Hear us in the name of our blessed Lord. Amen. (Source: Congressional Record- House, 87th Congress, second session, 108/9, Thursday, July 5, 1962, 12703.)

The opening of legislative sessions with prayer is embedded deeply into the tradition and history of our Country. From our founding era through the War for Independence, the practice of legislative prayer has been interwoven into the fabric of our culture and goes hand and glove with religious freedom. The connection of prayer and the U.S. Congress is undeniable and continues to this day. It is a reminder, along with our National motto "In God We Trust" that we should rely upon God to direct our efforts to govern this Nation. "Righteousness exalteth a nation: But sin is a reproach to any people" (Proverbs 14:34).

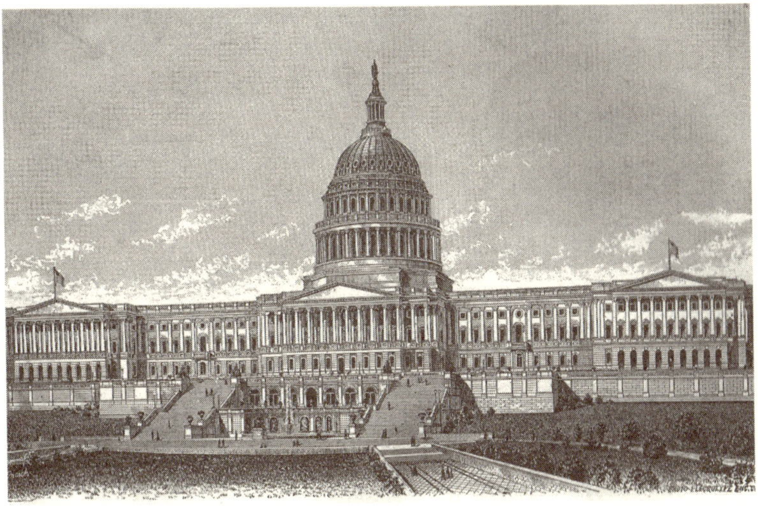

Chapter Five

Presidential Prayers

Webster's Dictionary defines an oath as "a solemn affirmation or declaration, made with an appeal to God for the truth of what is affirmed."

Article II, Section 1 of the United States Constitution states, "I solemnly swear that I will faithfully execute the office of the President of the United States, and will to the best of my ability, preserve, protect, and defend the Constitution of the United States."

Every President of our Country has sworn this oath. President George Washington added these words, "So help me, God." All Presidents who followed George Washington have emulated his addition.

Our Presidents have hailed from a wide variety of backgrounds: from veterans to venerated politicians, from businessmen to statesmen. All have placed their hand on the Bible and recited an oath that ended in a prayer; "So help me, God."

As our Presidents have voiced this prayer, so did King Solomon in the Holy Bible implore the King of kings, "Give therefore thy servant an understanding heart to judge thy people, that I may discern between good and bad: for who is able to judge this thy so great a people?" (1 Kings 3:9).

George Washington

A Prayer for Guidance

O eternal and everlasting God, I presume to present myself this morning before thy Divine majesty, beseeching thee to accept of my humble and hearty thanks, that it hath pleased thy great goodness to keep and preserve me the night past from all the dangers poor mortals are subject to, and has given me sweet and pleasant sleep, whereby I find my body refreshed and comforted for performing the duties of this day, in which I beseech thee to defend me from all perils of body and soul. Direct my thoughts, words and work, wash away my sins in the immaculate blood of the lamb, and purge my heart by thy holy spirit, from the dross of my natural corruption, that I may with more freedom of mind and liberty of will serve thee, the ever lasting God, in righteousness and holiness this day, and all the days of my life. Increase my faith in the sweet promises of the gospel; give me repentance from dead works; pardon my wanderings, and direct my thoughts unto thyself, the God of my salvation; teach me how to live in thy fear, labor in thy service, and ever to run in the ways of thy commandments; make me always watchful over my heart, that neither the terrors of conscience, the loathing of holy duties, the love of sin, nor an unwillingness to depart this life, may cast me into a spiritual slumber, but daily frame me more and more into the likeness of thy son Jesus Christ, that living in thy fear, and dying in thy favor, I may in thy appointed time attain the resurrection of the just unto eternal life bless my family, friends, and kindred. Unite us all in praising and glorifying thee in all our works begun, continued, and ended, when we shall come to make our last account before thee, blessed Saviour, who hath taught us thus to pray, "Our Father, who art in heaven, hallowed be preserve, protect and defend the Constitution of the United States." Increase my *faith* in the sweet promises of the gospel; give me repentance from dead works; pardon my wanderings, and direct my thoughts unto thyself, the God of my salvation; teach me how to live in thy fear, labor in thy service, and ever to run in the ways of thy commandments; make me always watchful over my heart, that neither the terrors of conscience, the loathing of holy duties, the love of sin, nor an unwillingness to depart this life, may cast me into a *spiritual* slumber, but daily frame me more and more into the likeness of thy son Jesus Christ, that living in thy fear, and dying in thy favor, I may in thy appointed time attain the resurrection of the just unto eternal life bless my family, friends, and kindred.

G Washington

~An undated prayer from Washington's prayer journal, Mount Vernon

John Adams

A Prayer for Success

May that Being who is supreme over all, the Patron of Order, the Fountain of Justice, and the Protector in all ages of the world of virtuous liberty, continue His blessing upon this nation and its Government and give it all possible success and duration consistent with the ends of His providence. I pray Heaven to bestow the best of blessing on this house, and on all that shall hereafter inhabit it. May none but honest and wise men ever rule under this roof!

John Adams

~From his inaugural address, March 4, 1797, and a prayer from a letter to his wife, November 2, 1800

Thomas Jefferson

A Prayer for the Nation

May that Infinite Power which rules the destinies of the universe lead our councils to what is best, and give them a favorable issue for your peace and prosperity.... I shall need, too, the favor of the Being in whose hands we are, who led our forefathers, as Israel of old, from their native land and planted them in a country flowing with all the necessities and comforts of life; who has covered our infancy with His Providence and our riper years with His wisdom and power, and to whose goodness I ask you to join with me in supplications that He will so enlighten the minds of your servants, guide their councils, and prosper their measures that whatever they do shall result in your good, and shall secure to you the peace, friendship, and approbation of all nations. Almighty God, Who has given us this good land for our heritage; We humbly beseech Thee that we may always prove ourselves a people mindful of Thy favor and glad to do Thy will. Bless our land with honorable ministry, sound learning, and pure manners. Save us from violence, discord, and confusion, from pride and arrogance, and from every evil way. Defend our liberties, and fashion into one united people the multitude brought hither out of many kindreds and tongues. Endow with Thy spirit of wisdom those to whom in Thy name we entrust the authority of government, that there may be justice and peace at home, and that through obedience to Thy law, we may show forth Thy praise among the nations of the earth. In time of prosperity fill our hearts with thankfulness, and in the day of trouble, suffer not our trust in Thee to fail; all of which we ask through Jesus Christ our Lord. Amen.

~Washington D.C., March 4, 1801

James Madison

A Prayer for Fellow Citizens

The source to which I look or the aids which alone can supply my deficiencies is in the well-tried intelligence and virtue of my fellow-citizens, and in the counsels of those representing them in the other departments associated in the care of the national interests. In these my confidence will under every difficulty be best placed, next to that which we have all been encouraged to feel in the guardianship and guidance of that Almighty Being whose power regulates the destiny of nations, whose blessings have been so conspicuously dispensed to this rising Republic, and to whom we are bound to address our devout gratitude for the past, as well as our fervent supplications and best hopes for the future.

James Madison

~Composed for his inauguration ceremonies, March 4, 1809

John Quincy Adams

A Prayer of Thanksgiving

May I never cease to be grateful for the numberless blessings received through life at His hands, never repine at what He has denied, never murmur at the dispensations of Providence, and implore His forgiveness for all the errors and delinquencies of my life! . . . I shall look for whatever success may attend my public service; and knowing that "except the Lord keep the city, the watchman waketh but in vain," with fervent supplications for His favor, to His overruling providence I commit with humble but fearless confidence my own fate and the future destinies of my country.

John Quincy Adams

~From his inaugural address, March 4, 1825

James Monroe

A Prayer for Protection

I enter on the trust to which I have been called by the suffrages of my fellow-citizens with my fervent prayers to the Almighty that He will be graciously pleased to continue to us that protection which He has already so conspicuously displayed in our favor. Beyond that I only look to the gracious protection of the Divine Being whose strengthening support I humbly solicit, and whom I fervently pray to look down upon us all. May it be among the dispensations of His providence to bless our beloved country with honors and with length of days. May her ways be ways of pleasantness and all her paths be peace! Today, I ask your prayers that in the years ahead I may have God's help in making decisions that are right for America, and I pray for your help so that together we may be worthy of our challenge. Let us go forward from here confident in hope, strong in our faith in one another, sustained by our faith in God who created us, and striving always to serve His purpose.

~James Monroe, March 4, 1817

John Tyler

A Prayer of Devotion

When a Christian people feel themselves to be overtaken by a great public calamity, it becomes them to humble themselves under the dispensation of Divine Providence to recognize His righteous government over the children of men, to acknowledge His goodness in time past, as well as their own unworthiness, and to supplicate His merciful protection for the future. We are all called upon by the highest obligations of duty to renew our thanks and our devotion to our Heavenly Parent, who has continued to vouchsafe to us the eminent blessings which surround us and who has so signally crowned the year with His goodness. If we find ourselves increasing beyond example in numbers, in strength, in wealth, in knowledge, in everything which promotes human and social happiness, let us ever remember our dependence for all these on the protection and merciful dispensations of Divine Providence.

John Tyler

~Prayer on the death of William Henry Harrison, April 13, 1841, and in Tyler's first public speech as President, December 7, 1841

James Knox Polk

A Prayer for Wisdom

In assuming responsibilities so vast I fervently invoke the aid of that Almighty Ruler of the Universe in whose hands are the destinies of nations and of men to guard this Heaven-favored land against the mischiefs which without His guidance might arise from an unwise public policy. With a firm reliance upon the wisdom of Omnipotence to sustain and direct me in the path of duty which I am appointed to pursue, I stand in the presence of this assembled multitude of my countrymen to take upon myself the solemn obligation "to the best of my ability to preserve, protect, and defend the Constitution of the United States." Confidently relying upon the aid and assistance of the coordinate departments of the Government in conducting our public affairs, I enter upon the discharge of the high duties which have been assigned me by the people, again humbly supplicating that Divine Being who has watched over and protected our beloved country from its infancy to the present hour to continue His gracious benedictions upon us, that we may continue to be a prosperous and happy people.

~James Knox Polk

Millard Fillmore

A Prayer during Calamity

I rely upon Him who holds in His hands the destinies of nations to endow me with the requisite strength for the task and to avert from our country the evils apprehended from the heavy calamity which has befallen us. God knows I detest slavery. I have no hostility to foreigners . . . having witnessed their deplorable condition in the old country. God forbid I should add to their sufferings by refusing them an asylum in this. And now, fellow-citizens, I can not bring this communication to a close without invoking you to join me in humble and devout thanks to the Great Ruler of Nations for the multiplied blessings which He has graciously bestowed upon us. His hand, so often visible in our preservation, had stayed the pestilence, saved us from foreign wars and domestic disturbances, and scattered plenty throughout the land. Our liberties, religious and civil, have been maintained, the fountains of knowledge have all been kept open, and means of happiness widely spread and generally enjoyed greater than have fallen to the lot of any other nation. And while deeply penetrated with gratitude for the past, let us hope that His all-wise providence will so guide our counsels as that they shall result in giving satisfaction to our constituents, securing the peace of the country, and adding new strength to the united Government under which we live. Our grateful thanks are due to an all-merciful Providence, not only for staying the pestilence which in different forms has desolated some of our cities, but for crowning the labors of the husbandman with an abundant harvest and the nation generally with the blessings of peace and prosperity.

Millard Fillmore

~*From his annual messages to Congress, December 2, 1850, and December 6, 1852*

A Prayer for Aid

Today I leave you; I go to assume a task more difficult than that which devolved upon General Washington. Unless the great God who assisted him shall be with and aid me, I must fail. But if the same omniscient mind, and the same Almighty arm that directed and protected him, shall guide and support me, I shall not fail, I shall succeed. Let us all pray that the God of our fathers may not forsake us now. To Him I commend you all— permit me to ask that with equal sincerity and faith you all will invoke His wisdom and guidance for me. Fondly do we hope, fervently do we pray, that this mighty scourge of war may speedily pass away. Yet, if God wills that it continue until all the wealth piled by the bondsman's two hundred and fifty years of unrequited toil shall be sunk, and until every drop of blood drawn with the lash shall be paid by another drawn with the sword, as was said three thousand years ago, so still it must be said "the judgments of the Lord are true and righteous altogether."

A. Lincoln

~Prayers shared on his leaving for Washington on February 12, 1861, and at his second inaugural, March 4, 1865

Abraham Lincoln

A Prayer for Peace

Fondly do we hope, fervently do we pray, that this mighty scourge of war may speedily pass away. Yet if God wills that it continues...until every drop of blood drawn with the lash shall be paid another drawn with the sword... so still it must be said that the judgments of the Lord are true and righteous altogether.

With malice toward none, with charity for all, with firmness in the right as God gives us to see the right, let us finish the work we are in, to bind up the nation's wounds, to care for him who shall have borne the battle, and for his widow and for his orphans, to do all which may achieve and cherish a just and a lasting peace among ourselves and with all nations.

~Second inaugural address, March 4, 1865

Ulysses S. Grant

A Prayer for Strength

All that I can do is to pray that the prayers of all those good people may be answered so far as to have us all meet in another and better world. I cannot speak even in a whisper. I pray God however that I may be spared to complete the necessary work...Should I die there will be a funeral and a break-up here. The review of the book for the printers will be suspended until fall. The subscriptions are so large that it can not be got out at the stipulated time even if there is no detention. But for these considerations I would welcome the arrival of the "Messenger of Peace," the earlier the better.

~From his letters, July 9, 1855

Rutherford B. Hayes

A Prayer for Safety

We want a united country. And if the great trust shall devolve upon me, I fervently pray that the Divine Being, who holds the destinies of the nations in his hands, will give me wisdom to perform its duties so as to promote the truest and best interests of the whole country. O Lord our Heavenly Father, who has safely brought us to the beginning of this day; defend us in the same with Thy Almighty power. Grant that we may not fall into any kind of danger and keep us from evil. May all our doings be ordered by Thy governance so that all we do may be righteous in Thy sight. Amen.

Rutherford B. Hayes

~A prayer recited by President Hayes and his wife each morning while he was in office, 1877-1880

James A. Garfield

A Prayer for Our Leaders

And now, fellow-citizens, I am about to assume the great trust which you have committed to my hands. I appeal to you for that earnest and thoughtful support which makes this Government in fact, as it is in law, a government of the people. I shall greatly rely upon the wisdom and patriotism of Congress and of those who may share with me the responsibilities and duties of administration, and, above all, upon our efforts to promote the welfare of this great people and their Government I reverently invoke the support and blessings of Almighty God. Now, more than ever before, the people are responsible for the character of their Congress. If that body be ignorant, reckless, and corrupt, it is because the people tolerate ignorance, recklessness, and corruption. If it be intelligent, brave, and pure, it is because the people demand these high qualities to represent them in the national legislature. . . If the next centennial does not find us a great nation. . . it will be because those who represent the enterprise, the culture, and the morality of the nation do not aid in controlling the political forces.

James A. Garfield

~Inauguration day, 1881

Chester A. Arthur

A Prayer of Blessings

𝕴t has long been the pious custom of our people, with the closing of the year, to look back upon the blessings brought to them in the changing course of the seasons and to return solemn thanks to the all-giving source from whom they flow. And although at this period, when the falling leaf admonishes us that the time of our sacred duty is at hand, our nation still lies in the shadow of a great bereavement, and the mourning which has filled our hearts still finds its sorrowful expression toward that God before whom we but lately bowed in grief and supplication, yet the countless benefits which have showered upon us during the past twelve-month call for our fervent gratitude and make it fitting that we should rejoice with thankfulness that the Lord in His infinite mercy has most signally favored our country and our people. Peace without and prosperity within have been vouchsafed to us, no pestilence has visited our shores, the abundant privileges of freedom which our fathers left us in their wisdom are still our increasing heritage; and if in parts of our vast domain sore affliction has visited our brethren in their forest homes, yet even this calamity has been tempered and in a manner sanctified by the generous compassion for the sufferers which has been called forth throughout our land. For all these things it is meet that the voice of the nation should go up to God in devout homage. Wherefore, I, Chester A. Arthur, President of the United States, do recommend that all the people observe Thursday, the 24th day of November instant, as a day of national thanksgiving and prayer, by ceasing, so far as may be, from their secular labors and meeting in their several places of worship, there to join in ascribing honor and praise to Almighty God, whose goodness has been so manifest in our history and in our lives, and offering earnest prayers that His bounties may continue to us and to our children.

~From his Thanksgiving proclamation, November 4, 1881

Grover Cleveland

A Prayer of Faith

We are unable to protect ourselves without aid, and therefore pray for the protection of the United States forces. Let us not trust to human effort alone, but humbly acknowledging the power and goodness of Almighty God, who presides over the destiny of nations, and who has at all times been revealed in our country's history, let us invoke His aid and His blessings upon our labors. Above all, I know there is a Supreme Being who rules the affairs of men and whose goodness and mercy have always followed the American people, and I know He will not turn from us now if we humbly and reverently seek His powerful aid.

Grover Cleveland

~Written from Washington, D.C., December 18, 1893, and March 4, 1885; found in his personal papers

William Henry Harrison

Prayers for Unity

To the good Being who has blessed us by the gifts of civil and religious freedom, who watched over and prospered the labors of our fathers and has hitherto preserved to us institutions far exceeding in excellence those of any other people, let us unite in fervently commending every interest of our beloved country in all future time. Entering thus solemnly into covenant with each other, we may reverently invoke and confidently expect the favor and help of Almighty God— that He will give to me wisdom, strength, and fidelity, and to our people a spirit of fraternity and a love of righteousness and peace.

~From their inaugural addresses, March 4, 1841, and March 4, 1889

Theodore Roosevelt

A Prayer for Charity

During the past year we have been free from famine, from pestilence, from war. We are at peace with all the rest of mankind. Our natural resources are at least as great as those of any other nation. We believe that in ability to develop and take advantage of these resources the average man of this nation stands at least as high as the average man of any other. Nowhere else in the world is there such an opportunity for a free people to develop to the fullest extent all its powers of body, of mind, and of that which stands above both body and mind— character. Much has been given us from on high, and much will rightly be expected of us in return. Into our care the ten talents have been entrusted, and we are to be pardoned neither if we squander and waste them, nor yet if we hide them in a napkin; for they must be fruitful in our hands. Ever throughout the ages, at all times and among all peoples, prosperity has been fraught with danger, and it behooves us to beseech the Giver of all things that we may not fall into loss of ease and luxury; that we may not lose our sense of moral responsibility; that we may not forget our duty to God and to our neighbor. A great democracy like ours, a democracy based upon the principles of orderly liberty, can be perpetuated only if in the heart of ordinary citizens there dwells a keen sense of righteousness and justice. We earnestly pray that this spirit of righteousness and justice may grow in the hearts of all of us, and that our souls may be inclined ever more both toward the virtues that tell for gentleness and tenderness, for loving-kindness and forbearance, one toward another, and toward those no less necessary virtues that make for manliness and rugged hardihood; for without these qualities neither nation nor individual can rise to the level of greatness. Now therefore, I, Theodore Roosevelt, President of the United States . . . recommend that the people shall cease from their daily work, and in their homes or in their churches, meet devoutly to thank the Almighty for the many and great blessings they have received in the past, and to pray that they may be given the strength so to order their lives as to deserve a continuation of these blessings in the future.

Theodore Roosevelt

~*Washington, D.C., October 26, 1907*

Calvin Coolidge

A Prayer for High Ideals

Here stands our country, an example of tranquility at home, a patron of tranquility abroad. Here stands its Government, aware of its might but obedient to its conscience. Here it will continue to stand, seeking peace and prosperity, solicitous for the welfare of the wage earner, promoting enterprise, developing waterways and natural resources, attentive to the intuitive counsel of womanhood, encouraging education, desiring the advancement of religion, supporting the cause of justice and honor among the nations. America seeks no earthly empire built on blood and dominions. The legions which she sends forth are armed, not with the sword, but with the cross. The higher state to which she seeks the allegiance of all mankind is not of human, but of divine origin. She cherishes no purpose save to merit the favor of Almighty God. There is in the soul of the nation a reserve for responding to the call to high ideals, to nobility of action, which has never yet been put forth. There is no problem so great but that somewhere a man is being raised up to meet it. There is no moral standard so high that the people cannot be raised up to it. God rules, and from the Bethlehems and the Springfields He sends them forth, His own, to do His work. In them we catch a larger gleam of the Infinite.

~From his inaugural address, March 4, 1925, and a speech in honor of Abraham Lincoln, February 12, 1922

Franklin D. Roosevelt

A Prayer in Dark Times

Almighty God: Our sons, pride of our nation, this day have set upon a mighty endeavor, a struggle to preserve our Republic, our religion and our civilization, and to set free a suffering humanity...

Lead them straight and true; give strength to their arms, stoutness to their hearts, steadfastness in their faith. They will need Thy blessings. Their road will be long and hard. For the enemy is strong. He may hurl back our forces. Success may not come with rushing speed, but we shall return again and again; and we know by Thy grace, and by the righteousness of our cause, our sons will triumph...

Embrace these, Father, and receive them, Thy heroic servants, into Thy kingdom. And for us at home--fathers, mothers, children, wives, sisters, and brothers of brave men overseas, whose thoughts and prayers are ever with them--help us, Almighty God, to rededicate ourselves in renewed faith in Thee in this hour of great sacrifice... Give us strength, too--strength in our daily tasks, to redouble the contributions we make in the physical and the material support of our armed forces.

With Thy blessing, we shall prevail over the unholy forces of our enemy. Help us to conquer the apostles of greed and racial arrogances. Lead us to the saving of our country, and with our sister nations into a world unity that will spell a sure peace--a peace invulnerable to the schemings of unworthy men. And a peace that will let all men live in freedom, reaping the just rewards of their honest toil.

~*D-Day, June 6, 1944*

Harry S. Truman

A Prayer for God's Will

At this moment, I have in my heart a prayer. As I have assumed my heavy duties, I humbly pray, Almighty God, in the words of King Solomon: "Give therefore thy servant an understanding heart to judge thy people, that I may discern between good and bad: for who is able to judge this thy so great a people?" I ask only to be a good and faithful servant of my Lord and my people. We can all pray. We all should pray. We should ask the fulfillment of God's will. We should ask for courage, wisdom, for the quietness of soul which comes alone to them who place their lives in His hands. Oh! Almighty and Everlasting God, Creator of Heaven, Earth, and the Universe, help me to be, to think, to act what is right, because it is right; make me truthful, honest, and honorable in all things; make me intellectually honest for the sake of right and honor and without thought of reward to me. Give me the ability to be charitable, forgiving, and patient with my fellowmen— help me to understand their motives and their shortcomings— even as Thou understandest mine! Amen, Amen, Amen.

~Harry S. Truman

Dwight Eisenhower

A Prayer for Our Leaders

Almighty God, as we stand here at this moment my future associates in the executive branch of government join me in beseeching that Thou will make full and complete our dedication to the service of the people in this throng, and their fellow citizens everywhere. Give us, we pray, the power to discern clearly right from wrong, and allow all our words and actions to be governed thereby, and by the laws of this land. Especially we pray that our concern shall be for all the people regardless of station, race, or calling. May cooperation be permitted and be the mutual aim of those who, under the concepts of our Constitution, hold to differing political faiths; so that all may work for the good of our beloved country and Thy glory. Before all else, we seek, upon our common labor as a nation, the blessings of Almighty God. And the hopes in our hearts fashion the deepest prayers of our whole people. May we pursue the right— without self-righteousness. May we know unity— without conformity. May we grow in strength— without pride in self. May we, in our dealings with all peoples of the earth, ever speak and serve justice.

And so shall America-in the sight of all men of good will-prove true to the honorable purposes that bind and rule us as a people in all this time of trial through which we pass.

~Prayers from his two inaugural addresses, January 20, 1953, and January 21, 1957

Ronald Reagan

A Prayer for Healing

To preserve our blessed land we must look to God... It is time to realize that we need God more than He needs us... We also have His promise that we could take to heart with regard to our country, that "If my people, which are called by my name shall humble themselves, and pray and seek my face, and turn from their wicked ways; then I will hear from heaven and will forgive their sin, and will heal their land."

Let us, young and old, join together, as did the First Continental Congress, in the first step, in humble heartfelt prayer. Let us do so for the love of God and His great goodness, in search of His guidance and the grace of repentance, in seeking His blessings, His peace, and the resting of His kind and holy hands on ourselves, our nation, our friends in the defense of freedom, and all mankind, now and always.

The time has come to turn to God and reassert our trust in Him for the healing of America... Our country is in need of and ready for a spiritual renewal. Today, we utter no prayer more fervently than the ancient prayer for peace on Earth.

If I had a prayer for you today, among those that have all been uttered, it is that one we're so familiar with: "The Lord bless you and keep you; the Lord make His face to shine upon you and be gracious unto you; the Lord lift up His countenance upon you and give you peace...." And God bless you all.

Ronald Reagan

~From a speech to the American people, February 6, 1986

George H. W. Bush

A Prayer to Help Others

My first act as President is a prayer. I ask you to bow your heads.

Heavenly Father, we bow our heads and thank You for Your love. Accept our thanks for the peace that yields this day and the shared faith that makes its continuance likely. Make us strong to do Your work, willing to heed and hear Your will, and write on our hearts these words: "Use power to help people." For we are given power not to advance our own purposes, nor to make a great show in the world, nor a name. There is but one just use of power, and it is to serve people. Help us to remember it, Lord.

The Lord our God be with us, as He was with our fathers; may He not leave us or forsake us; so that He may incline our hearts to Him, to walk in all His ways... that all peoples of the earth may know that the Lord is God; there is no other.

~Inaugural address, January 20, 1989

Chapter Six

Present-Day Prayers

The Promise for America

There are many people who ask us how they can pray effectively for America. In an effort to assist anyone who would ask that question, we have compiled a list of verses and prayers. When we see there is a need for healing in our land, God gives us a way in the Holy Bible we can call upon Him for help.

"If my people, which are called by my name, shall humble themselves, and pray, and seek my face, and turn from their wicked ways; then will I hear from heaven, and will forgive their sin, and will heal their land" (2 Chronicles 7:14).

To begin, we have explained the various aspects of 2 Chronicles 7:14:

It is a national promise with a prerequisite attached. The words "if" and "then" refer to the two aspects of this verse.

The word "if" shows that the children of God must:

1.Humble themselves.

If we humble ourselves He will hear us. Humility is an indispensable part of praying for our Country. If we are proud, God will resist us.

"But he giveth more grace. wherefore He saith, God resisteth the proud, but giveth grace unto the humble" (James 4:6).

2. Pray.

Prayer is obeying God.

"Continue in prayer, and watch in the same with thanksgiving" (Colossians 4:2).

"Watch ye therefore, and pray always, that ye may be accounted worthy to escape all these things that shall come to pass, and to stand before the Son of man" (Luke 21:36).

3. Seek God's face.

Seeking God's face is a daily commitment.

"Yet they seek me daily, and delight to know my ways, as a nation that did righteousness, and forsook not the ordinance of their God: they ask of me the ordinances of justice; they take delight in approaching to God" (Isaiah 58:2).

We must determine to pray for our Nation and God's mercy upon us each and every day. Some may say this will take great determination. The answer is we will pray for our Nation in one of two ways, **either out of determination or out of desperation.**

4. Turn from their wicked ways.

"If I regard iniquity in my heart, the Lord will not hear me" (Psalm 66:18).

The word "then" shows that God will:

1. Hear from heaven.

God answers prayer.

"Call unto me, and I will answer thee, and shew thee great and mighty things, which thou knowest not" (Jeremiah 33:3).

"And all things, whatsoever ye shall ask in prayer, believing, ye shall receive" (Matthew 21:22).

2. Forgive their sins.

God is a God of mercy

"For thou, Lord, art good, and ready to forgive; and plenteous in mercy unto all them that call upon thee" (Psalm 86:5).

3. Heal their land.

Divine intercession is the hope for America.

The Prayers for America

These Scriptural prayers are addressed to the LORD of the Holy Bible.

1. Our Nation deserves judgment, but we ask You for Your forgiveness and mercy.

"Ah sinful nation, a people laden with iniquity, a seed of evildoers, children that are corrupters: they have forsaken the Lord, they have provoked the Holy One of Israel unto anger, they are gone away backward" (Isaiah 1:4).

"But thou shalt say unto them, This is a nation that obeyeth not the voice of the Lord their God, nor receiveth correction: truth is perished, and is cut off from their mouth" (Jeremiah 7:28).

"But thou, O Lord, art a God full of compassion, and gracious, longsuffering, and plenteous in mercy and truth" (Psalms 86:15).

"The Lord is merciful and gracious, slow to anger, and plenteous in mercy" (Psalms 103:8).

"Let us therefore come boldly unto the throne of grace, that we may obtain mercy, and find grace to help in time of need" (Hebrews 4:16).

"And forgive us our sins; for we also forgive every one that is indebted to us. And lead us not into temptation; but deliver us from evil" (Luke 11:4).

2. Forgive our Nation for the sin of idolatry and for turning our hearts away from You, the only true and living God.

"But the Lord is the true God, he is the living God, and an everlasting king: at his wrath the earth shall tremble, and the nations shall not be able to abide his indignation" (Jer. 10:10).

"And go not after other gods to serve them, and to worship them, and provoke me not to anger with the works of your hands; and I will do you no hurt" (Jer. 25:6).

"Repent, and turn yourselves from your idols; and turn away your faces from all your abominations" (Ezekiel 14:6b).

"Because Ephraim hath made many altars to sin, altars shall be unto him to sin" (Hosea 8:11).

"Now while Paul waited for them at Athens, his spirit was stirred in him, when he saw the city wholly given to idolatry" (Acts. 17:16).

"Wherefore, my dearly beloved, flee from idolatry" (1 Cor. 10:14).

"For they themselves shew of us what manner of entering in we had unto you, and how ye turned to God from idols to serve the living and true God" (1 Thess.1:9).

3. Forgive our Nation for being a forgetful people.

"Of the Rock that begat thee thou art unmindful, and hast forgotten God that formed thee" (Deut. 32:18).

"For they have perverted their way, and they have forgotten the Lord their God" (Jer. 3:21b).

"Remember the former things of old: for I am God, and there is none else; I am God, and there is none like me" (Isaiah 46:9).

"According to their pasture, so were they filled; they were filled, and their heart was exalted; therefore have they forgotten me" (Hosea13:6).

4. Protect our Nation from our enemies and deliver us from evil within and without.

"Have not I commanded thee? Be strong and of a good courage; be not afraid, neither be thou dismayed: for the Lord thy God is with thee whithersoever thou goest" (Joshua 1:9).

"The wicked flee when no man pursueth: but the righteous are bold as a lion" (Prov. 28:1).

"But they that wait upon the Lord shall renew their strength; they shall mount up with wings as eagles; they shall run, and not be weary; and they shall walk, and not faint" (Isa. 40:31).

"Fear thou not; for I am with thee: be not dismayed; for I am thy God: I will strengthen thee; yea, I will help thee; yea, I will uphold thee with the right hand of my righteousness" (Isa. 41:10).

"Peace I leave with you, my peace I give unto you: not as the world giveth, give I unto you. Let not your heart be troubled, neither let it be afraid" (John 14:27).

"These things I have spoken unto you, that in me ye might have peace. In the world ye shall have tribulation: but be of good cheer; I have overcome the world" (John 16:33).

"We are troubled on every side, yet not distressed; we are perplexed, but not in despair; Persecuted, but not forsaken; cast down, but not destroyed" (2 Cor. 4:8-9).

"This know also, that in the last days perilous times shall come" (2 Tim. 3:1).

"Wherefore take unto you the whole armour of God, that ye may be able to withstand in the evil day, and having done all, to stand" (Eph. 6:13).

"But and if ye suffer for righteousness' sake, happy are ye: and be not afraid of their terror, neither be troubled" (1 Peter 3:14).

7. Spare our Nation for the sake of the very small remnant of faithful believers in You.

"Except the Lord of Hosts had left unto us a very small remnant, we should have been as Sodom, and we should have been like unto Gomorrah" (Isa. 1:9).

8. Help our Nation to turn to righteousness, postponing Your judgment.

"If that nation, against whom I have pronounced, turn from their evil, I will repent of the evil that I thought to do unto them" (Jeremiah 18:8).

"Therefore now amend your ways and your doings, and obey the voice of the Lord your God; and the Lord will repent him of the evil that he hath pronounced against you" (Jeremiah 26:13).

"Righteousness exalteth a nation: but sin is a reproach to any people" (Prov. 14:34).

9. Help us to be more informed, to be more involved, and to intercede in prayer for our Nation.

"And of the children of Issachar, which were men that had understanding of the times, to know what Israel ought to do" (1 Chron.12:32).

"And he spake a parable unto them to this end, that men ought always to pray, and not to faint" (Luke 18:1).

"Pray without ceasing. In every thing give thanks: for this is the will of God in Christ Jesus concerning you" (1 Thess 5:17-18).

"The effectual fervent prayer of a righteous man availeth much" (James 5:16b).

10. Awaken us from our complacency and move us to action; challenge us and give us a renewed vision and a burden for our Country. Illuminate our minds and hearts.

"And where there is no vision, the people perish" (Prov. 29:18).

"Awake to righteousness, and sin not; for some have not the knowledge of God: I speak this to your shame" (1 Cor. 15:34).

"The eyes of your understanding being enlightened; that ye may know what is the hope of his calling, and what the riches of the glory of his inheritance in the saints" (Eph. 1:18).

11. Help us to shine as lights in the world and renew a fire within our hearts that we will burn brightly for You. Forgive us for being lukewarm.

"That ye may be blameless and harmless, the sons of God, without rebuke, in the midst of a crooked and perverse nation, among whom ye shine as lights in the world" (Phil. 2:15).

"Let your light so shine before men, that they may see your good works, and glorify your Father which is in heaven" (Matt. 5:16).

"And of the angels he saith, Who maketh his angels spirits, and his ministers a flame of fire" (Heb. 1:7).

"I know thy works, that thou art neither cold nor hot: I would thou wert cold or hot. So then because thou art lukewarm, and neither cold nor hot, I will spue thee out of my mouth" (Rev. 3:15-16).

12. We want to stand in the gap for our Country so You will not destroy it.

"And I sought for a man among them, that should make up the hedge, and stand in the gap before me for the land, that I should not destroy it: but I found none" (Ezekiel 22:30).

13. Help us to be the salt of the earth.

"Ye are the salt of the earth: but if the salt have lost his savour, wherewith shall it be salted? It is thenceforth good for nothing, but to be cast out, and to be trodden under foot of men" (Matt. 5:13).

14. Please bring our Nation back to where you can bless us.

"Blessed is the nation whose God is the Lord; and the people whom he hath chosen for his own inheritance" (Ps. 33:12).

"When the righteous are in authority, the people rejoice: but when the wicked beareth rule, the people mourn" (Prov. 29:2).

15. Help our Nation to be people of understanding and knowledge so You can prolong our peace, prosperity and liberty.

"For the transgression of a land many are the princes thereof: but by a man of understanding and knowledge the state thereof shall be prolonged" (Prov. 28:2).

16. We know our future looks dark, but we know You still sit on the throne of eternity, and with You all things are possible.

"And Jesus looking upon them saith, With men it is impossible, but not with God: for with God all things are possible" (Mark 10:27).

17. We know You are the ruler over all the earth and in control of our very lives. We pray for Thy will to be done.

"He ruleth by his power for ever; his eyes behold the nations: let not the rebellious exalt themselves" (Psalms 66:7).

"The Lord hath prepared his throne in the heavens; and his kingdom ruleth over all" (Psalms 103:19).

"And we know that all things work together for good to them that love God, to them who are the called according to his purpose" (Ro. 8:28).

"Thy kingdom come. Thy will be done in earth, as it is in heaven" (Matt. 6:10).

18. Help us to put our trust in You.

"But let all those that put their trust in thee rejoice: let them ever shout for joy, because thou defendest them: let them also that love thy name be joyful in thee" (Psalms 5:11).

"What time I am afraid, I will trust in thee" (Psalms 56:3).

"In God have I put my trust: I will not be afraid what man can do unto me" (Psalms 56:11).

"It is better to trust in the Lord than to put confidence in man" (Psalms 56:11).

"Trust in the Lord with all thine heart; and lean not unto thine own understanding. In all thy ways acknowledge him, and he shall direct thy paths" (Prov. 3:5-6).

"The Lord is good, a strong hold in the day of trouble; and he knoweth them that trust in him" (Prov. 3:5-6).

19. Stir us to get involved in government to see it as a call from you. We need people who will govern our Nation by Biblical principles, who fear You, and who will stand up for what is right.

"The God of Israel said, the Rock of Israel spake to me, he that ruleth over men must be just, ruling in the fear of God" (I2 Sam. 23:3).

"Moreover thou shalt provide out of all the people able men, such as fear God, men of truth, hating covetousness; and place such over them, to be rulers of thousands, and rulers of hundreds, rulers of fifties, and rulers of tens" (Ex. 18:21).

20. Thank You for America as it is still the greatest Nation on earth. Thank You for our freedom, liberty and justice.

21. Help us to watch and to pray for Your return and allow us to occupy until You come.

"And he called his ten servants, and delivered them ten pounds, and said unto them, Occupy till I come" (Luke 19:13).

"Take ye heed, watch and pray: for ye know not when the time is" (Mark 13:33).

"Watch ye therefore, and pray always, that ye may be accounted worthy to escape all these things that shall come to pass, and to stand before the Son of man" (Luke 21:36).

"I must work the works of him that sent me, while it is day: the night cometh, when no man can work" (John 9:4).

"Therefore, my beloved brethren, be ye stedfast, unmoveable, always abounding in the work of the Lord, forasmuch as ye know that your labour is not in vain in the Lord" (1 Cor. 15:58).

"But whoso looketh into the perfect law of liberty, and continueth therein, he being not a forgetful hearer, but a doer of the work, this man shall be blessed in his deed" (James 1:25).

The Prayers for America's Leaders

Hear us as we pray for our National leaders as 1Timothy 2:1-5 exhorts.

"I exhort therefore, that, first of all, supplications, prayers, intercessions, and giving of thanks, be made for all men; for kings, and for all that are in authority; that we may lead a quiet and peaceable life in all godliness and honesty. for this is good and acceptable in the sight of God our savior. who will have all men to be saved, and to come unto the knowledge of the truth. for there is one God, and one mediator between God and men, the man Christ Jesus;"

President
Vice President
President's Cabinet
Cabinet Rank Members

Supreme Court Justices

Senators
Congressmen

State & Local Government Officials

<u>Department of Defense</u>
United States Army
United States Navy
United States Marines
United States Air Force
United States Coast Guard
Military Intelligence

<u>Department of Homeland Security</u>
National Security Agency
Central Intelligence Agency
Federal Bureau of Investigation

"But that which ye have already hold fast till I come" (Rev. 2: 25).

"Surely I come quickly. Amen. Even so, come, Lord Jesus" (Rev. 22:20).

Chapter Seven

Patterns for Prayers

Specific Prayers God Desires

As Jesus teaches His disciples in the Sermon on the Mount, He reveals a model prayer which many people call the Lord's Prayer. In this prayer, Jesus reveals different elements we should include in our prayers.

1. We are to pray to our Father. (Is God your Father?) John 1:12
2. We are to glorify and reverence His name.
3. We are to pray for the soon fulfillment of God's kingdom on earth.
4. We are to pray for God's will to be done in our lives. Romans 12:2
5. We are to pray for our daily (bread) sustenance.
6. We are to pray for God's mercy and forgiveness.
7. We are to pray for God's deliverance from evil.

"After this manner therefore pray ye: Our Father which art in heaven, Hallowed be thy name. Thy kingdom come. Thy will be done in earth, as it is in heaven. Give us this day our daily bread. And forgive us our debts, as we forgive our debtors. And lead us not into temptation, but deliver us from evil: For thine is the kingdom, and the power, and the glory, for ever. Amen. For if ye forgive men their trespasses, your heavenly Father will also forgive you" (Matthew 6:9–14).

"And this is the confidence that we have in him, that, if we ask any thing according to his will, he heareth us" (1 John 5:14).

Consecrated Prayers God Desires

God desires His child to be clean spiritually when he or she prays. Notice the words from the following verse, *turn from their wicked ways*. We must confess our sins to God and then seek His face.

"If my people, which are called by my name, shall humble themselves, and pray, and seek my face, and turn from their wicked ways; then will I hear from heaven, and will forgive their sin, and will heal their land" (2 Chronicles 7:14).

"If I regard iniquity in my heart, The Lord will not hear me" (Psalm 66:18).

"If we confess our sins, he is faithful and just to forgive us our sins, and to cleanse us from all unrighteousness" (1 John 1:9).

"Confess your faults one to another, and pray one for another, that ye may be healed. The effectual fervent prayer of a righteous man availeth much" (James 5:16).

Personal Prayers God Desires

Jesus admonished His disciples to pray to God and not to pray to be seen of men. The setting Jesus recommends to His disciples is one of personal seclusion (closet) and is a setting with which Jesus Himself was very familiar.

"And when thou prayest, thou shalt not be as the hypocrites are: for they love to pray standing in the synagogues and in the corners of the streets, that they may be seen of men. Verily I say unto you, They have their reward. But thou, when thou prayest, enter into thy closet, and when thou hast shut thy door, pray to thy Father which is in secret; and thy Father which seeth in secret shall reward thee openly" (Matthew 6:5–6).

Corporate Prayers God Desires

In the book of Acts, God's people came together in the corporate fashion to pray for Peter who was in prison, and God answered their prayers.

"Peter therefore was kept in prison: but prayer was made without ceasing of the church unto God for him. And when Herod would have brought him forth, the same night Peter was sleeping between two soldiers, bound with two chains: and the keepers before the door kept the prison. And, behold, the angel of the Lord came upon him, and a light shined in the prison: and he smote Peter on the side, and raised him up, saying, Arise up quickly. And his chains fell off from his hands. And the angel said unto him, Gird thyself, and bind on thy sandals. And so he did. And he saith unto him, Cast thy garment about thee, and follow me" (Acts 12:5–8).

Intercessory Prayers God Desires

Our Country as well as our leaders must be prayed for every day of the year. The Bible is very clear in its teachings concerning prayer in 1Timothy 2:1-6.

The diamond of prayer has many facets. Notice the different types of prayers.

1. Supplications - specific requests
2. Prayers - sincere prayers to God
3. Intercessions - prayer on behalf of others
4. Giving of thanks - prayers thanking God for His dealings

As we practice the facet of intercessory prayer we are instructed who we should pray for:

1. Pray for all men
2. Pray for kings or presidents
3. Pray for all in authority
4. Pray for all men to be saved

"I exhort therefore, that, first of all, supplications, prayers, intercessions, *and* giving of thanks, be made for all men; For kings, and for all that are in authority; that we may lead a quiet and peaceable life in all godliness and honesty. For this is good and acceptable in the sight of God our Saviour; Who will have all men to be saved, and to come unto the knowledge of the truth. For there is one God, and one mediator between God and men, the man Christ Jesus; Who gave himself a ransom for all, to be testified in due time" (1Timothy 2:1–6).

The Word of God also reveals the truth of how the spiritual world goes into action when the believer prays. In the book of Daniel, we clearly see God's child (Daniel) pray, and we see the angels of heaven involved in spiritual warfare on Daniel's behalf.

"And he said unto me, O Daniel, a man greatly beloved, understand the words that I speak unto thee, and stand upright: for unto thee am I now sent. And when he had spoken this word unto me, I stood trembling. Then said he unto me, Fear not, Daniel: for from the first day that thou didst set thine heart to understand, and to chasten thyself before thy God, **thy words were heard**, and I am come for thy words" (Daniel 10:11–12).

God hears His child's prayers and will answer His child's prayers. Sometimes God answers *yes*, sometimes God answers *no*, other times God answers *wait*. In all prayers, we must understand God will always do His will.

Chapter Eight

Personal Prayers

OF PRAYER.

"Evening, and morning, and at noon will I pray."—PSALMS.

I WILL rise and pray while the dews of morn,
Like gems are scattered o'er tree and thorn,
Ere the sun comes up, in his glorious bower,
To waken the bird and open the flower;
I will turn from earth, to Heaven aspiring,
With faith unshaken, hope untiring,
And for strength to walk through the weary day,
To the God of love will I kneel and pray.

I will pray at noon, when the fervid glow
Of the sultry sun is upon my brow;
When the flocks have sought the shading trees;
When the stream is silent, and hushed the breeze;
And praise the doings of nature's God;
Then closing my eyes on the glorious day,
To the God of love will I kneel and pray.

I will pray at eve, when the crimson light
Is passing away from the mountain's height;
When the holy, solemn twilight hour
Is hushing the bird and closing the flower;
When all is rest, and the stars come forth
To keep their watch o'er the sleeping earth—
To Him who hath kept, and blest through the day,
To the God of love will I kneel and pray.

Thus will I pray, for I find it sweet
To be often found at my Maker's feet;
I will always pray—on the heavenly road—
I ne'er shall faint while I lean on my God.
I shall gather strength for my upward flight;
My path will be as the shining light;
It shall heighten to perfect, eternal day
Therefore to God will I always pray.

ANONYMOUS.

Personal Prayers from the Bible

Sunday

FOR HELP

"Hear me when I call, O God of my righteousness thou hast enlarged me when I was in distress; have mercy upon me, and hear my prayer" (Psalm 4:1).

"Give ear to my words, O Lord, consider my meditation. Hearken unto the voice of my cry, my King, and my God: for unto thee will I pray. My voice shalt thou hear in the morning, O Lord; in the morning will I direct my prayer unto thee, and will look up" (Psalm 5:1-3).

"Let the words of my mouth, and the meditation of my heart, be acceptable in thy sight, O Lord, my strength, and my redeemer" (Psalm 19:14).

FOR MERCY AND FORGIVENESS

"O Lord, rebuke me not in thine anger, neither chasten me in thy hot displeasure. Have mercy upon me, O Lord; for I am weak" (Psalm 6:1-2a).

"For thy name's sake, O Lord, pardon mine iniquity; for it is great" (Psalm 25:11).

"Look upon mine affliction and my pain; and forgive all my sins" (Psalm 25:18).

"It is of the Lord's mercies that we are not consumed, because his compassions fail not. They are new every morning: great is thy faithfulness. The Lord is my portion, saith my soul; therefore will I hope in him. The Lord is good unto them that wait for him, to the soul that seeketh him" (Lamentations 3:22-25).

FOR GUIDANCE

"Lead me, O Lord, in thy righteousness because of mine enemies; make thy way straight before my face" (Psalm 5:8).

"Thou wilt shew me the path of life: in thy presence is fulness of joy; at thy right hand there are pleasures for evermore" (Psalm 16:11).

"For thy lovingkindness is before mine eyes: and I have walked in thy truth" (Psalm 26:3).

FOR ENCOURAGEMENT

"Thou hast proved mine heart; thou hast visited me in the night; thou hast tried me, and shalt find nothing; I am purposed that my mouth shall not transgress" (Psalm 17:3).

"Let integrity and uprightness preserve me; for I wait on thee" (Psalm 25:21).

"Wait on the Lord: be of good courage, and he shall strengthen thine heart: wait, I say, on the Lord" (Psalm 27:14).

"Thy words were found, and I did eat them; and thy word was unto me the joy and rejoicing of mine heart: for I am called by thy name, O Lord God of hosts" (Jer. 15:16).

FOR PRAISE

"I will praise the Lord according to his righteousness: and will sing praise to the name of the Lord most high" (Psalm 7:17).

"O Lord our Lord, how excellent is thy name in all the earth! who hast set thy glory above the heavens" (Psalm 8:1).

"I will praise thee, O Lord, with my whole heart; I will shew forth all thy marvellous works. I will be glad and rejoice in thee: I will sing praise to thy name, O thou most High" (Psalm 9:1-2).

As for me, I will behold thy face in righteousness: I shall be satisfied, when I awake, with thy likeness" (Psalm 17:15).

"I will call upon the Lord, who is worthy to be praised: so shall I be saved from mine enemies" (Psalm 18:3).

"To the end that my glory may sing praise to thee, and not be silent. O Lord my God, I will give thanks unto thee for ever" (Psalm 30:12).

"Forasmuch as there is none like unto thee, O Lord; thou art great, and thy name is great in might" (Jer. 10:6).

FOR PROTECTION

"O Lord my God, in thee do I put my trust: save me from all them that persecute me, and deliver me" (Psalm 7:1).

"Preserve me, O God: for in thee do I put my trust" (Psalm 16:1).

"Keep me as the apple of the eye, hide me under the shadow of thy wings, From the wicked that oppress me, from my deadly enemies, who compass me about" (Psalm 17:8).

"Unto thee, O Lord, do I lift up my soul. O my God, I trust in thee: let me not be ashamed, let not mine enemies triumph over me" (Psalm 25:1-2).

"O Lord, thou knowest: remember me, and visit me, and revenge me of my persecutors; take me not away in thy longsuffering: know that for thy sake I have suffered rebuke" (Jer. 15:15).

FOR OTHERS

"Shew thy marvellous lovingkindness, O thou that savest by thy right hand them which put their trust in thee from those that rise up against them" (Psalm 17: 7).

FOR INSTRUCTION

"I will bless the Lord, who hath given me counsel: my reins also instruct me in the night seasons. I have set the Lord always before me: because he is at my right hand, I shall not be moved. Therefore my heart is glad, and my glory rejoiceth: my flesh also shall rest in hope"(Psalm 16:7-9).

"I will instruct thee and teach thee in the way which thou shalt go: I will guide thee with mine eye" (Psalm 32:8).

"Remember the former things of old: for I am God, and there is none else; I am God, and there is none like me, Declaring the end from the beginning, and from ancient times the things that are not yet done, saying, My counsel shall stand, and I will do all my pleasure" (Isaiah 46:9-10).

Monday

FOR HELP

"Examine me, O Lord, and prove me; try my reins and my heart" (Psalm 26:2).

"Hear, O Lord, when I cry with my voice: have mercy also upon me, and answer me" (Psalm 27:7).

"Hear, O Lord, and have mercy upon me: Lord, be thou my helper" (Psalm 30:10).

FOR MERCY AND FORGIVENESS

"Remember, O Lord, thy tender mercies and thy lovingkindnesses; for they have been ever of old. Remember not the sins of my youth, nor my transgressions: according to thy mercy remember thou me for thy goodness 'sake, O Lord" (Psalm 25:6-7).

"Thy mercy, O Lord, is in the heavens; and thy faithfulness reacheth unto the clouds" (Psalm 36:5).

"Deliver me from all my transgressions: make me not the reproach of the foolish" (Psalm 39: 8).

"I said, Lord, be merciful unto me: heal my soul; for I have sinned against thee" (Psalm 41:4).

FOR GUIDANCE

"Shew me thy ways, O Lord; teach me thy paths. Lead me in thy truth, and teach me: for thou art the God of my salvation; on thee do I wait all the day" (Psalm 25:4-5).

"Teach me thy way, O Lord, and lead me in a plain path, because of mine enemies" (Psalm 27:11).

"Thus saith the Lord, thy Redeemer, the Holy One of Israel; I am the Lord thy God which teacheth thee to profit, which leadeth thee by the way that thou shouldest go" (Isaiah 48:17).

FOR ENCOURAGEMENT

"Judge me, O Lord; for I have walked in mine integrity: I have trusted also in the Lord; therefore I shall not slide" (Psalm 26:1).

"And now, Lord, what wait I for? my hope is in thee" (Psalm 39:7).

FOR PRAISE

"The Lord is my strength and my shield; my heart trusted in him, and I am helped: therefore my heart greatly rejoiceth; and with my song will I praise him" (Psalm 28:7).

"Give unto the Lord the glory due unto his name; worship the Lord in the beauty of holiness" (Psalm 29:2).

"Sing unto the Lord, O ye saints of his, and give thanks at the remembrance of his holiness" (Psalm 30:4).

"Be glad in the Lord, and rejoice, ye righteous: and shout for joy, all ye that are upright in heart" (Psalm 32:11).

"I will bless the Lord at all times: his praise shall continually be in my mouth" (Psalm 34:1).

"O taste and see that the Lord is good: blessed is the man that trusteth in him" (Psalm 34:8).

"And my tongue shall speak of thy righteousness and of thy praise all the day long" (Psalm 35:28).

"Many, O Lord my God, are thy wonderful works which thou hast done, and thy thoughts which are to us-ward: they cannot be reckoned up in order unto thee: if I would declare and speak of them, they are more than can be numbered" (Psalm 40:5).

"Let all those that seek thee rejoice and be glad in thee: let such as love thy salvation say continually, The Lord be magnified" (Psalm 40:16).

"O Lord, open thou my lips; and my mouth shall shew forth thy praise" (Psalm 51:15).

FOR PROTECTION

"Turn thee unto me, and have mercy upon me; for I am desolate and afflicted. The troubles of my heart are enlarged: O bring thou me out of my distresses" (Psalm 25:16-17).

"O keep my soul, and deliver me: let me not be ashamed; for I put my trust in thee" (Psalm 25: 20).

"Deliver me not over unto the will of mine enemies: for false witnesses are risen up against me, and such as breathe out cruelty" (Psalm 27:12).

"In thee, O Lord, do I put my trust; let me never be ashamed: deliver me in thy righteousness" (Psalm 31:1).

FOR OTHERS

"Let the lying lips be put to silence; which speak grievous things proudly and contemptuously against the righteous" (Psalm 31:18).

FOR INSTRUCTION

"Be still, and know that I am God: I will be exalted among the heathen, I will be exalted in the earth" (Psalm 46:10).

Tuesday

FOR HELP

"Forsake me not, O Lord: O my God, be not far from me. Make haste to help me, O Lord my salvation" (Psalm 38:21-22).

"Hear my prayer, O Lord, and give ear unto my cry; hold not thy peace at my tears: for I am a stranger with thee, and a sojourner, as all my fathers were. O spare me, that I may recover strength, before I go hence, and be no more" (Psalm 39:13).

"Hear my prayer, O God; give ear to the words of my mouth" (Psalm 54:2).

FOR MERCY AND FORGIVENESS

"But as for me, I will walk in mine integrity: redeem me, and be merciful unto me" (Psalm 26:11).

"Have mercy upon me, O God, according to thy lovingkindness: according unto the multitude of thy tender mercies blot out my transgressions. Wash me throughly from mine iniquity, and cleanse me from my sin. For I acknowledge my transgressions: and my sin is ever before me. Against thee, thee only, have I sinned, and done this evil in thy sight: that thou mightest be justified when thou speakest, and be clear when thou judgest" (Psalm 51:1-4).

FOR GUIDANCE

"For thou art my rock and my fortress; therefore for thy name's sake lead me, and guide me" (Psalm 31: 3).

"Lord, make me to know mine end, and the measure of my days, what it is; that I may know how frail I am" (Psalm 39:4).

FOR ENCOURAGEMENT

"How excellent is thy lovingkindness, O God therefore the children of men put their trust under the shadow of thy wings" (Psalm 36:7).

"I waited patiently for the Lord; and he inclined unto me, and heard my cry. He brought me up also out of an horrible pit, out of the miry clay, and set my feet upon a rock, and established my goings. And he hath put a new song in my mouth, even praise unto our God: many shall see it, and fear, and shall trust in the Lord" (Psalm 40:1-3).

"I delight to do thy will, O my God: yea, thy law is within my heart" (Psalm 40:8).

"As the hart panteth after the water brooks, so panteth my soul after thee, O God" (Psalm 42:1).

"For my thoughts are not your thoughts, neither are your ways my ways, saith the Lord. For as the heavens are higher than the earth, so are my ways higher than your ways, and my thoughts than your thoughts" (Isaiah 55:8-9).

FOR PRAISE

'Be thou exalted, O God, above the heavens; let thy glory be above all the earth" (Psalm 57:5).

"Because thy lovingkindness is better than life, my lips shall praise thee. Thus will I bless thee while I live: I will lift up my hands in thy name. My soul shall be satisfied as with marrow and fatness; and my mouth shall praise thee with joyful lips" (Psalm 63:3-5).

FOR PROTECTION

"Bow down thine ear to me; deliver me speedily: be thou my strong rock, for an house of defence to save me" (Psalm 31:2).

"Pull me out of the net that they have laid privily for me: for thou art my strength" (Psalm 31:4).

"But I trusted in thee, O Lord: I said, Thou art my God. My times are in thy hand: deliver me from the hand of mine enemies, and from them that persecute me" (Psalm 31:14-15).

"Plead my cause, O Lord, with them that strive with me: fight against them that fight against me" (Psalm 35:1).

"God is our refuge and strength, a very present help in trouble" (Psalm 46:1).

"Therefore will not we fear, though the earth be removed, and though the mountains be carried into the midst of the sea; Though the waters thereof roar and be troubled, though the mountains shake with the swelling thereof" (Psalm 46:2-3).

"And call upon me in the day of trouble: I will deliver thee, and thou shalt glorify me" (Psalm 50:15).

FOR OTHERS

"O continue thy lovingkindness unto them that know thee; and thy righteousness to the upright in heart" (Psalm 36:10).

FOR INSTRUCTION

"Delight thyself also in the Lord; and he shall give thee the desires of thine heart" (Psalm 37:4).

"Rest in the Lord, and wait patiently for him: fret not thyself because of him who prospereth in his way, because of the man who bringeth wicked devices to pass" (Psalm 37:7).

Wednesday

FOR HELP

"Hear my cry, O God; attend unto my prayer"(Psalm 61:1).

"Hear me, O Lord; for thy lovingkindness is good: turn unto me according to the multitude of thy tender mercies" (Psalm 69:16).

"But I am poor and needy: make haste unto me, O God: thou art my help and my deliverer; O Lord, make no tarrying" (Psalm 70:5).

FOR MERCY AND FORGIVENESS

"Withhold not thou thy tender mercies from me, O Lord: let thy lovingkindness and thy truth continually preserve me" (Psalm 40:11).

"But thou, O Lord, art a God full of compassion, and gracious, longsuffering, and plenteous in mercy and truth" (Psalm 86:15).

FOR GUIDANCE

"Teach me thy way, O Lord; I will walk in thy truth unite my heart to fear thy name" (Psalm 86:11).

"So teach us to number our days, that we may apply our hearts unto wisdom" (Psalm 90:12).

FOR ENCOURAGEMENT

"O God, thou art my God; early will I seek thee: my soul thirsteth for thee, my flesh longeth for thee in a dry and thirsty land, where no water is" (Psalm 63:1).

"My soul longeth, yea, even fainteth for the courts of the Lord: my heart and my flesh crieth out for the living God" (Psalm 84:2).

"O Lord, thou hast searched me, and known me. Thou knowest my downsitting and mine uprising, thou understandest my thought afar off" (Psalm 139:1-2).

FOR PRAISE

"Whoso offereth praise glorifieth me: and to him that ordereth his conversation aright will I shew the salvation of God" (Psalm 50:23).

"Let my mouth be filled with thy praise and with thy honour all the day" (Psalm 71:8).

"For thou art great, and doest wondrous things thou art God alone" (Psalm 86:10).

"I will praise thee, O Lord my God, with all my heart: and I will glorify thy name for evermore" (Psalm 86:12).

"O Lord, how great are thy works! and thy thoughts are very deep" (Psalm 92:5).

FOR PROTECTION

"Be pleased, O Lord, to deliver me: O Lord, make haste to help me" (Psalm 40:13).

"Judge me, O God, and plead my cause against an ungodly nation: O deliver me from the deceitful and unjust man" (Psalm 43:1).

"When I cry unto thee, then shall mine enemies turn back: this I know; for God is for me" (Psalm 56:9).

"In God have I put my trust: I will not be afraid what man can do unto me" (Psalm 56:11).

"What time I am afraid, I will trust in thee" (Psalm 56:3).

"Be merciful unto me, O God, be merciful unto me: for my soul trusteth in thee: yea, in the shadow of thy wings will I make my refuge, until these calamities be overpast" (Psalm 57:1).

"Deliver me from mine enemies, O my God: defend me from them that rise up against me" (Psalm 59:1).

FOR OTHERS

"Do good, O Lord, unto those that be good, and to them that are upright in their hearts" (Psalm 125:4).

FOR INSTRUCTION

"As for me, I will call upon God; and the Lord shall save me. Evening, and morning, and at noon, will I pray, and cry aloud: and he shall hear my voice" (Psalm 55:16-17).

"Cast thy burden upon the Lord, and he shall sustain thee: he shall never suffer the righteous to be moved" (Psalm 55:22).

"Trust in him at all times; ye people, pour out your heart before him: God is a refuge for us" (Psalm 62:8).

"Thus saith the Lord, Stand ye in the ways, and see, and ask for the old paths, where is the good way, and walk therein, and ye shall find rest for your souls" (Jer. 6:16 a).

Thursday

FOR HELP

"Bow down thine ear, O Lord, hear me: for I am poor and needy" (Psalm 86:1).

"Be merciful unto me, O Lord: for I cry unto thee daily" (Psalm 86:3).

"Give ear, O Lord, unto my prayer; and attend to the voice of my supplications" (Psalm 86:6).

FOR MERCY AND FORGIVENESS

"Create in me a clean heart, O God; and renew a right spirit within me. Cast me not away from thy presence; and take not thy holy spirit from me. Restore unto me the joy of thy salvation; and uphold me with thy free spirit" (Psalm 51:10-12).

"Let, I pray thee, thy merciful kindness be for my comfort, according to thy word unto thy servant. Let thy tender mercies come unto me, that I may live: for thy law is my delight" (Psalm 119:76-77).

FOR GUIDANCE

"Teach me, O Lord, the way of thy statutes; and I shall keep it unto the end" (Psalm 119:33).

"Teach me good judgment and knowledge: for I have believed thy commandments" (Psalm 119:66).

FOR ENCOURAGEMENT

"When I remember thee upon my bed, and meditate on thee in the night watches. Because thou hast been my help, therefore in the shadow of thy wings will I rejoice. My soul followeth hard after thee: thy right hand upholdeth me" (Psalm 63:6-8).

"Thou compassest my path and my lying down, and art acquainted with all my ways. For there is not a word in my tongue, but, lo, O Lord, thou knowest it altogether. Thou hast beset me behind and before, and laid thine hand upon me" (Psalm 139:3-5).

FOR PRAISE

"We have thought of thy lovingkindness, O God, in the midst of thy temple. According to thy name, O God, so is thy praise unto the ends of the earth: thy right hand is full of righteousness" (Psalm 48:9).

"It is a good thing to give thanks unto the Lord, and to sing praises unto thy name, O most High: To shew forth thy lovingkindness in the morning, and thy faithfulness every night" (Psalm 92:1-2).

"But thou, Lord, art most high for evermore" (Psalm 92:8).

"O Lord, how manifold are thy works! in wisdom hast thou made them all: the earth is full of thy riches" (Psalm 104:24).

"O God, my heart is fixed; I will sing and give praise, even with my glory" (Psalm 108:1).

"Be thou exalted, O God, above the heavens: and thy glory above all the earth" (Psalm 108:5).

FOR PROTECTION

"Unto thee, O my strength, will I sing: for God is my defense, and the God of my mercy" (Psalm 59:17).

"From the end of the earth will I cry unto thee, when my heart is overwhelmed: lead me to the rock that is higher than I. For thou hast been a shelter for me, and a strong tower from the enemy. I will abide in thy tabernacle for ever: I will trust in the covert of thy wings" (Psalm 61:2-4).

"Hear my voice, O God, in my prayer: preserve my life from fear of the enemy" (Psalm 64:1).

"In the day of my trouble I will call upon thee for thou wilt answer me" (Psalm 86: 7).

"But whoso hearkeneth unto me shall dwell safely, and shall be quiet from fear of evil" (Prov. 1:33).

FOR OTHERS

"But I say unto you, Love your enemies, bless them that curse you, do good to them that hate you, and pray for them which despitefully use you, and persecute you" (Matthew 5:44).

FOR INSTRUCTION

"If I regard iniquity in my heart, the Lord will not hear me" (Psalm 66:18).

"But it is good for me to draw near to God: I have put my trust in the Lord God, that I may declare all thy works" (Psalm 73:28).

"Let us come before his presence with thanksgiving, and make a joyful noise unto him with psalms" (Psalm 95:2).

"O come, let us worship and bow down: let us kneel before the Lord our maker" (Psalm 95:6).

"O worship the Lord in the beauty of holiness: fear before him, all the earth" (Psalm 96:9).

"Rejoice in the Lord, ye righteous; and give thanks at the remembrance of his holiness" (Psalm 97:12).

"Thus saith the Lord, Let not the wise man glory in his wisdom, neither let the mighty man glory in his might, let not the rich man glory in his riches: But let him that glorieth glory in this, that he understandeth and knoweth me, that I am the Lord which exercise lovingkindness, judgment, and righteousness, in the earth: for in these things I delight, saith the Lord" (Jer. 9:23-24).

Friday

FOR HELP

"Hear my prayer, O Lord, and let my cry come unto thee" (Psalm 102:1).

"Hear my voice according unto thy lovingkindness: O Lord, quicken me according to thy judgment" (Psalm 119:149).

FOR MERCY AND FORGIVENESS

"Purge me with hyssop, and I shall be clean: wash me, and I shall be whiter than snow" (Psalm 51:7).

"O God, thou knowest my foolishness; and my sins are not hid from thee" (Psalm 69:5).

FOR GUIDANCE

"I am thy servant; give me understanding, that I may know thy testimonies" (Psalm 119:125).

"Order my steps in thy word: and let not any iniquity have dominion over me" (Psalm 119:133).

FOR ENCOURAGEMENT

"Rejoice the soul of thy servant: for unto thee, O Lord, do I lift up my soul" (Psalm 86: 4).

"O how love I thy law! it is my meditation all the day" (Psalm 119:97).

"How precious also are thy thoughts unto me, O God! how great is the sum of them! If I should count them, they are more in number than the sand: when I awake, I am still with thee" (Psalm 139:17-18).

"I the Lord search the heart, I try the reins, even to give every man according to his ways, and according to the fruit of his doings" (Jer 17:10).

FOR PRAISE

"For ever, O Lord, thy word is settled in heaven" (Psalm 119:89).

"Righteous art thou, O Lord, and upright are thy judgments" (Psalm 119:137).

"Unto thee lift I up mine eyes, O thou that dwellest in the heavens" (Psalm 123:1).

"I will worship toward thy holy temple, and praise thy name for thy lovingkindness and for thy truth: for thou hast magnified thy word above all thy name" (Psalm 138:2).

FOR PROTECTION

"Shew me a token for good; that they which hate me may see it, and be ashamed: because thou, Lord, hast holpen me, and comforted me" (Psalm 86: 17).

"But do thou for me, O God the Lord, for thy name's sake: because thy mercy is good, deliver thou me" (Psalm 109:21).

"Help me, O Lord my God: O save me according to thy mercy: That they may know that this is thy hand; that thou, Lord, hast done it" (Psalm 109:26-27).

"All thy commandments are faithful: they persecute me wrongfully; help thou me" (Psalm 119:86).

FOR OTHERS

"And when ye stand praying, forgive, if ye have ought against any: that your Father also which is in heaven may forgive you your trespasses" (Mark 11:25).

FOR INSTRUCTION

"Make a joyful noise unto the Lord, all the earth: make a loud noise, and rejoice, and sing praise" (Psalm 98:4).

"Exalt the Lord our God, and worship at his holy hill; for the Lord our God is holy" (Psalm 99:9).

"Make a joyful noise unto the Lord, all ye lands. Serve the Lord with gladness: come before his presence with singing. Know ye that the Lord he is God: it is he that hath made us, and not we ourselves; we are his people, and the sheep of his pasture. Enter into his gates with thanksgiving, and into his courts with praise: be thankful unto him, and bless his name. For the Lord is good; his mercy is everlasting; and his truth endureth to all generations" (Psalm 100:1-5).

"I love them that love me; and those that seek me early shall find me" (Prov. 8:17).

Saturday

FOR HELP

"Lord, hear my voice: let thine ears be attentive to the voice of my supplications" (Psalm 130:2).

"Search me, O God, and know my heart: try me, and know my thoughts: And see if there be any wicked way in me, and lead me in the way everlasting" (Psalm 139:23-24).

"Hear my prayer, O Lord, give ear to my supplications: in thy faithfulness answer me, and in thy righteousness" (Psalm 143:1).

FOR MERCY AND FORGIVENESS

"For thou, Lord, art good, and ready to forgive; and plenteous in mercy unto all them that call upon thee" (Psalm 86: 5).

"O satisfy us early with thy mercy; that we may rejoice and be glad all our days" (Psalm 90:14).

"Deliver my soul, O Lord, from lying lips, and from a deceitful tongue" (Psalm 120:2).

FOR GUIDANCE

"Set a watch, O Lord, before my mouth; keep the door of my lips" (Psalm 141:3).

"Teach me to do thy will; for thou art my God: thy spirit is good; lead me into the land of uprightness" (Psalm 143:10).

FOR ENCOURAGEMENT

"Thy testimonies are wonderful: therefore doth my soul keep them" (Psalm 119:129).

"I stretch forth my hands unto thee: my soul thirsteth after thee, as a thirsty land." (Psalm 143:6).

"For I know the thoughts that I think toward you, saith the Lord, thoughts of peace, and not of evil, to give you an expected end" (Jer. 29:11).

FOR PRAISE

"Oh that men would praise the Lord for his goodness, and for his wonderful works to the children of men" (Psalm 107:8).

"I will praise thee; for I am fearfully and wonderfully made: marvellous are thy works; and that my soul knoweth right well" (Psalm 139:14).

"I remember the days of old; I meditate on all thy works; I muse on the work of thy hands" (Psalm 143:5).

"I will speak of the glorious honour of thy majesty, and of thy wondrous works" (Psalm 145:5).

"Praise ye the Lord. Praise God in his sanctuary: praise him in the firmament of his power. Praise him for his mighty acts: praise him according to his excellent greatness" (Psalm 150:1-2).

"Let every thing that hath breath praise the Lord. Praise ye the Lord" (Psalm 150:6).

FOR PROTECTION

"Consider mine affliction, and deliver me: for I do not forget thy law. Plead my cause, and deliver me: quicken me according to thy word" (Psalm 119:153-154).

"Deliver me, O Lord, from the evil man: preserve me from the violent man" (Psalm 140:1).

"Grant not, O Lord, the desires of the wicked: further not his wicked device; lest they exalt themselves" (Psalm 140:8).

"Deliver me, O Lord, from mine enemies: I flee unto thee to hide me" (Psalm 143:9).

"Quicken me, O Lord, for thy name's sake: for thy righteousness 'sake bring my soul out of trouble" (Psalm 143:11).

FOR OTHERS

"Confess your faults one to another, and pray one for another, that ye may be healed. The effectual fervent prayer of a righteous man availeth much." (James 5:16).

FOR INSTRUCTION

"Seek the Lord, and his strength: seek his face evermore" (Psalm 105:4).

"O give thanks unto the Lord; for he is good: because his mercy endureth for ever" (Psalm 118:1).

"Pray for the peace of Jerusalem: they shall prosper that love thee" (Psalm 122:6).

"O give thanks unto the Lord; for he is good: for his mercy endureth for ever" (Psalm 136:1).

"Cause me to hear thy lovingkindness in the morning; for in thee do I trust: cause me to know the way wherein I should walk; for I lift up my soul unto thee" (Psalm 143:8).

"With my soul have I desired thee in the night; yea, with my spirit within me will I seek thee early: for when thy judgments are in the earth, the inhabitants of the world will learn righteousness" (Isa. 26:9).

"Call unto me, and I will answer thee, and shew thee great and mighty things, which thou knowest not" (Jeremiah 33:3).

Chapter Nine

Promissory Prayer

Promissory Prayer

- Jesus came into the world to save sinners.

"And she shall bring forth a son, and thou shalt call his name JESUS: for he shall save his people from their sins" (Matthew 1:21).

- Since all people are sinners, all people need Jesus Christ to save them.

"For all have sinned, and come short of the glory of God" (Romans 3:23).

- Jesus can save sinners because He died on the cross to pay for their sins and rose again from the dead to conquer *death*.

"But God commendeth his love toward us, in that, while we were yet sinners, Christ died for us" (Romans 5:8).

- Because Satan hates sinners, he does not want them to understand that Jesus alone can save them, so he blinds them to the true Gospel.

"But if our gospel be hid, it is hid to them that are lost: in whom the god of this world (Satan) hath blinded the minds of them which believe not, lest the light of the glorious gospel of Christ, who is the image of God, should shine unto them" (2 Corinthians 4:3,4).

- Satan has fooled people into believing they can be saved from their sins by something other than Christ's death on the cross.

- God's Word teaches that doing good works or being good cannot save you, and "...there is none that doeth good, no, not one" (Romans 3:12b).

"Not by works of righteousness which we have done, but according to his mercy he saved us" (Titus 3:5a).

"For by grace are ye saved through faith; and that not of yourselves: it is the gift of God: Not of works, lest any man should boast" (Ephesians 2:8,9).

- **God's Word teaches being religious (going to church) cannot save you.**

"Two men went up into the temple to pray; the one a Pharisee, and the other a publican. The Pharisee stood and prayed thus with himself, God, I thank thee, that I am not as other men are, extortioners, unjust, adulterers, or even as this publican. I fast twice in the week, I give tithes of all that I possess. And the publican, standing afar off, would not lift up so much as his eyes unto heaven, but smote upon his breast, saying, God be merciful to me a sinner. I tell you, this man went down to his house justified rather than the other: for every one that exalteth himself shall be abased; and he that humbleth himself shall be exalted" (Luke 18:10-14).

- **God will save you by giving you the gift of eternal life. A gift is not something you earn or deserve, but something you receive that was paid for by somebody else.**

"For the wages of sin is death; but the gift of God is eternal life through Jesus Christ our Lord" (Romans 6:23).

- **Salvation does not come by anything other than receiving Jesus Christ as your Lord and Savior.**

"But as many as received him, to them gave he power to become the sons of God, even to them that believe on his name" (John 1:12).

"And this is the record, that God hath given to us eternal life, and this life is in his Son. He that hath the Son hath life; and he that hath not the Son of God hath not life" (1 John 5:11,12).

- **If you understand and believe, then you can call upon Jesus at this very moment, and HE WILL SAVE YOUR SOUL.**

"For whosoever shall call upon the name of the Lord shall be saved" (Romans 10:13).

God wants to give you the best gift ever offered anyone. Why not accept the Lord Jesus Christ now? Will you pray this prayer?

O God...I know that I am a sinner...I am sorry for my sins...I know that Jesus Christ died on the cross, shed his blood to save me and rose again...I know that Jesus can save me and that He is the only one who can save me... and the best way I know how...I ask Jesus to come into my heart and save me now...Amen.

Sweet hour of prayer! sweet hour of prayer!
That calls me from a world of care,
And bids me at my Father's throne
Make all my wants and wishes known.
In seasons of distress and grief,
My soul has often found relief,
And oft escaped the tempter's snare,
By thy return, sweet hour of prayer!

Sweet hour of prayer! sweet hour of prayer!
The joys I feel, the bliss I share,
Of those whose anxious spirits burn
With strong desires for thy return!
With such I hasten to the place
Where God my Savior shows His face,
And gladly take my station there,
And wait for thee, sweet hour of prayer!

Sweet hour of prayer! sweet hour of prayer!
Thy wings shall my petition bear
To Him whose truth and faithfulness
Engage the waiting soul to bless.
And since He bids me seek His face,
Believe His Word and trust His grace,
I'll cast on Him my every care,
And wait for thee, sweet hour of prayer!

DR. CHUCK HARDING
Missionary Evangelist

Dr. Chuck Harding grew up in the Washington, D.C. area. God gave him the unique privilege of being the Deputy Commander of the Uniformed Protective Branch of the Diplomatic Security Service at the State Department. He is a student of history and has seen our government in action first-hand. He is able to provide effective governmental advice for pastors and churches and preaches God and Country meetings and Constitutional Awareness Conferences nationwide.

PASTOR T. MICHAEL CREED
Independent Baptist Church

Pastor T. Michael Creed grew up in a pastor's home in the greater Washington D.C. area. He has pastored the Independent Baptist Church of Clinton, Maryland for 19 years and has a desire to reach Capitol Hill for Christ. He has teamed up with Dr. Harding in an effort to help churches better understand the need for their involvement in governmental affairs.